lonely planet

POCKET

TORONTO

TOP SIGHTS · LOCAL EXPERIENCES

T0018355

LIZA PRADO

Contents

Plan Your Trip 4

CN Tower, designed by John Andrews (p44)
YELENA RODRIGUEZ MENA/EYEEM/GETTY IMAGES ©

Explore
Toronto 27

Worth a Trip

Survival
Guide 147

COVID-19

We have re-checked every business in this book before publication to ensure that it is still open after the COVID-19 outbreak. However, the economic and social impacts of COVID-19 will continue to be felt long after the outbreak has been contained, and many businesses, services and events referenced in this guide may experience ongoing restrictions. Some may be temporarily closed, have changed their opening hours and services, or require bookings; some unfortunately could have closed permanently. We suggest you check with venues before visiting for the latest information.

Top Experiences

Walk CN Tower's glass floor, 342m up...if you dare (p44)

Find the maker station at Art Gallery of Ontario (p92)

Graze the food stalls of St Lawrence Market Complex (p60)

Get drenched on a Niagara Falls boat tour (p142)

Catch a show at Elgin & Winter Garden Theatre (p76)

CLICK IMAGES/ALAMY STOCK PHOTO ©

LEFT: JHVEPHOTO/GETTY IMAGES ©. RIGHT: PUFFIN'S PICTURES/SHUTTERSTOCK ©

Enjoy a free festival at Harbourfront Centre (p30)

Go birdwatching in Tommy Thompson Park (p72) Pictured: Tree swallow

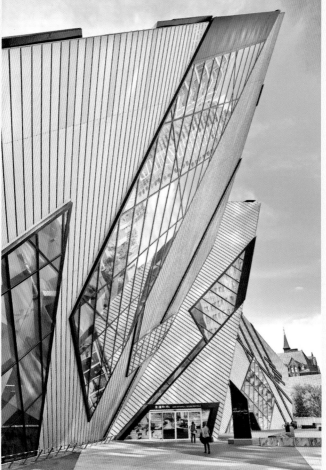

JAVEN/SHUTTERSTOCK ©; ARCHITECT DANIEL LIBESKIND

Discover fossils and skeletons at Royal Ontario Museum (p104)

See the city skyline from Toronto Islands (p40)

ROBERTO DESTARAC PHOTO/SHUTTERSTOCK ©

GABRIELESTOCKS/SHUTTERSTOCK ©

Join an eco-workshop at Evergreen Brick Works (p132)

CANADAPANDA/SHUTTERSTOCK ©

See the spring cherry blossoms in High Park (p118)

Dining Out

Nowhere is Toronto's multiculturalism more thrilling than in its restaurants. You'll find everything from Korean walnut cakes and sweat-inducing Thai curries to good ol' Canuck pancakes with peameal bacon and maple syrup. Fusion food is hot: traditional Western recipes are spiked with zingy Eastern ingredients, while British influences linger with fizzy lunchtime pints and formal afternoon tea.

Global Eats

Toronto has more than 7000 restaurants, representing a phenomenal range of tastes, cultures and experiences. Most neighborhoods are known for a certain scene – there's fine dining in the financial district, and hole-in-the-wall eats and homegrown talent in Kensington Market and Chinatown – but the truth is there's great food from around the world in every corner of Toronto. If ever there was a place to explore, graze and experiment, this is it.

Fine Dining

Toronto is deep into the fine dining and celebrity chef scene. Restaurants are stylish and exclusive, with idiosyncratic techniques and ingredients, and usually a menu of creative cocktails. A splurge perhaps, but always Instagram-worthy.

Food Halls

Can't decide what to eat or where to go? Dining halls may be the answer, featuring a variety of first-rate cuisines, with counter service and communal tables, and a relaxed but lively ambience. They're uber-popular and popping up all over town; Assembly Chef's Hall (pictured; p52) is a fine place to start.

Best Budget Eats

House of Gourmet No-frills restaurant with a dizzying number of Hong Kong–style dishes. (p96)

Seven Lives Standing-room-only place serving the best fish tacos in town. (p97)

Otto's Bierhalle Brats, beer and communal tables evoke Oktoberfest year-round. (p122)

EQROY/SHUTTERSTOCK ©

Annex Food Hall Industrial-chic food court with eateries from vegan to Bangkok-style street food. (p110)

Best Fine Dining

Buca Artisanal nose-to-tail Italian served in an upscale setting, soaring ceilings and all. (p53)

Lee Mid-century Modern–inspired dining room with creative Asian plates meant to be shared. (p53)

Ruby Watchco Different nightly menu of farm-to-table comfort food. (p140)

Richmond Station Streamlined restaurant with an eclectic menu of beautifully presented dishes. (p53)

Best Specialty Eats

Pow Wow Café Fry-bread tacos are the specialty at this cozy Ojibwe eatery. (p97)

Okonomi House Simple restaurant serving *okonomiyaki* (stuffed Japanese cabbage pancakes). (p83)

Chef's House Culinary students work the front and back of this upscale restaurant. (p67)

Dipped Donuts Tiny bakery serving fancy doughnuts with surprising toppings. (p98)

Show Time

As you might have guessed, there's always something going on in Toronto, from jazz and art-house cinema to offbeat theater, opera, punk rock, and hockey. In summer, free festivals and outdoor concerts are the norm, but Toronto's live-music scene keeps grooving year-round.

Theater

Long winter months indoors are conducive to the creation and performance of theatrical works. This, and Toronto's relative proximity to Broadway and cosmopolitan Montréal, help sustain the city's reputation as a theater-maker's playground. Broadway and off-Broadway musicals and plays pack theaters around the Entertainment District and Yonge & Dundas Sq. There are numerous smaller venues and vibrant young production companies around town too.

Live Music

Dust off your Iggy Pop T-shirt, don your Docs and hit the pit. Alt-rock, metal, ska, punk and funk – Toronto has a thriving live-music scene. Bebop, smoky swamp blues, classical and acoustic balladry provide some alternatives. Expect to pay anywhere from nothing to a few dollars on weeknights, up to $20 for weekend acts.

Ticketing

In an effort to promote arts and culture, many venues and events operate a 'Pay What You Can' (PWYC) policy: admission is free or by donation – give what you think is reasonable. Otherwise, Ticketmaster (www.ticketmaster.ca) sells tickets for major concerts, sporting matches and events.

Best Iconic Experiences

Elgin & Winter Garden Theatre Historic double-decker theater with big Broadway shows. (pictured; p76)

Horseshoe Tavern Legendary stage for indie bands. (p99)

Toronto Maple Leafs Fiery fans and sold-out games make watching the Leafs unforgettable. (p57)

COLIN WOODS/SHUTTERSTOCK ©

Best Live Music

Reservoir Lounge Longtime 'it' spot for jazz and blues. (p69)

Rex Nightly jazz and blues, from traditional to experimental. (p100)

Dakota Tavern Country-music joint with a sweet bluegrass brunch. (p126)

Best Theater

Royal Alexandra Theatre Impressive 1907 theater staging big-ticket musicals. (p56)

Soulpepper Theater company producing plays focused on the diversity of the Canadian experience. (p69)

Shakespeare in High Park Outdoor Shakespeare in one of Toronto's prettiest parks. (p119)

Best Cinemas

TIFF Bell Lightbox Magnificent cinema complex screening independent films year-round. (p55)

Hot Docs Ted Rogers Cinema Art deco theater showcasing documentaries and off-the-beaten-track films. (p113)

Entertainment Resources

blogTO (www.blogto.com) Up-to-date info on local happenings.

Now (nowtoronto.com) Alt-culture and live-music listings.

Tourism Toronto (www.seetorontonow.com) Official tourism website with events listings.

Bar Open

Toronto's drinking scene embraces everything from gritty dive bars to sky-high cocktail lounges, plus a clubbing scene that centers on the Entertainment District. Strict bylaws prohibit smoking indoors in public spaces, although some patios allow it. Taps start flowing around midday and last call hovers around 2am.

TRPHOTOS/SHUTTERSTOCK ©

Best Bars

Bar Raval Magnificent Gaudí-inspired bar serving small Spanish plates, too. (p124)

Oxley Upscale British pub with Victorian decor and glitzy clientele. (p112)

Drake Hotel Smart rooftop bar and hipster underground music venue in the West End. (p125)

O'Grady's Irish pub popular for its patio and its Dirty Bingo Nights, hosted by drag queens. (p86)

Best Breweries

Bellwoods Brewery Award-winning beers, gourmet small plates and a hipster vibe in a two-story brewery. (p124)

Rorschach Brewing Co Century-old house turned brewery, with two patios and an ever-changing menu of beers. (p73)

Mill Street Brewery Distillery District brewery in a Victorian-era factory with over a dozen craft brews on tap. (p68)

Best City Views

Rooftop Floor-to-ceiling windows and a wraparound patio on a, yes, spectacular rooftop. (p140)

One Eighty Glitzy bar with Toronto's highest licensed patio – 51 floors up! (p87)

Against the Grain Urban Tavern Lakefront views from a spacious patio. (p39)

Best Quirky & Unusual

Storm Crow Manor Sci-fi-themed bar with dungeon masters on staff. (p87)

Snakes & Lattes More than 1000 board games plus an eclectic drink menu. (p126)

Festivals

SHAWN GOLDBERG/SHUTTERSTOCK ©

Toronto loves festivals! Summer months are especially busy, but count on events year-round. Arts, food and culture festivals are especially popular, including the Toronto Film Festival and Pride Toronto. Others celebrate theater, music, neighborhoods, historical events and more. Check local calendars for festivals taking place during your stay.

Best Performing Arts Festivals

Toronto Fringe Festival (📞416-966-1062; http://fringetoronto.com; $13; ⏰early Jul) Theater festival featuring more than 150 productions chosen by lottery.

Luminato (📞416-368-4849; www.luminatofestival.com; ⏰Jun) Performing-arts and ideas festival featuring some of the world's top creatives.

Toronto Jazz Festival (📞416-928-2033; www.tojazz.com; ⏰late Jun; Michael Franti pictured above) Ten days of jazz, blues and soul, held everywhere from parks to concert halls.

Best Arts & Culture Festivals

Doors Open Toronto (www.toronto.ca/doorsopen; free; ⏰late May) Architecturally and historically significant buildings open their doors for public viewing one weekend a year.

International Festival of Authors (📞416-973-4000; www.readings.org;
York Quay, 235 Queens Quay W; from $20; ⏰late Oct) Acclaimed writers come for readings, talks, book signings and more.

Nuit Blanche Toronto (http://nbto.com; ⏰1st Sat Oct) One night, all night, of countless urban art experiences around town.

Foodie Festivals Summer

For a showcase of Toronto's culinary diversity, check out the prix fixe food fest of **Summerlicious** (p139) with hundreds of participating restaurants. For a more informal fest, head to **Union Summer** (p53) food market with gourmet food stalls, live music and outdoor film screenings.

Treasure Hunt

Shopping in Toronto is a big deal. When it's -20°C outside, you have to fill the gap between brunch and the movies with something, right? People like to update their wardrobes and redecorate their homes, or just walk around the sprawling Eaton Centre. This habit continues through to summer, making boutique-hopping an excuse to hit the streets.

KIEV.VICTOR/SHUTTERSTOCK ©

Best Souvenirs

Spacing Store *Spacing*-magazine gift shop with unique Toronto souvenirs, including ones showcasing particular neighborhoods. (p57)

Outer Layer Well-curated shop selling whimsical gifts and knickknacks from Toronto and Canada beyond. (p57)

Best Markets

St Lawrence Market Complex Classic Toronto market experience since the 1800s. (pictured; p60)

Sunday Antique Market Toronto's best antique market, set in St Lawrence Market Complex. (p61)

Best Art & Artisanal Works

Bay of Spirits Gallery Spectacular gallery showcasing indigenous Canadian art. (p101)

Craft Ontario Shop Longtime gallery-boutique specializing in works by Ontario-based artisans. (p127)

Arts Market Eclectic art collective featuring a unique items made by locals. (p141)

Best Books

Glad Day Oldest operating LGBTIQ+ bookstore on earth. (p88)

Type Books Charming independent bookstore with a top-notch children's-book section. (p128)

Shopping Tips

○ Save your shopping for Thursday and Friday evenings, when stores stay open late.

○ Mom-and-pop shops in Kensington Market and Chinatown often accept cash only.

○ Toronto applies 13% sales tax to all purchases.

Under the Radar

FANNY LELORRAIN/SHUTTERSTOCK ©

With so many offerings in Toronto's core, it's easy to overlook lesser known neighborhoods. But there are many opportunities for more of a locals' scene or off-the-beaten track experiences just a quick bus (or cab) ride away.

The Junction

The Junction – and by extension Junction Triangle – is one of Toronto's most vibrant up-and-coming neighborhoods. Named after four railway lines that meet here, the neighborhood was once a manufacturing community with foundries, meat packing plants and nail factories. Today these abandoned factories and warehouses are being re-purposed into galleries and museums, breweries and boho boutiques. The heart of the action is on Dundas Street West, and trail-blazers like the **Museum of Contemporary Art** (p122) and **Henderson Brewing Company** (p126) are just a stone's throw away.

The Beaches

The name says it all: the Beaches is a chilled-out neighborhood on Toronto's eastern shore. It's a place to stroll the boardwalk, dig your toes into the tawny sand, even brave the chilly lake waters on a hot summer day. Popular **Kew Beach** (cnr Lee Ave & boardwalk) has Adirondack chairs and even a fire pit that's lit on winter weekends (BYO marshmallows). When hunger strikes, Queen Street East is dotted with mom-and-pop eateries with robust 'to-go' offerings. Nearby **Woodbine Park** (1695 Queen St E) also hosts festivals like locals' fave **Beaches International Jazz Festival** (www.beachesjazz.com).

The GTA

The Greater Toronto Area (GTA) is also well worth exploring. Must-sees include:

McMichael Canadian Art Collection (10365 Islington Ave, Kleinburg; www.mcmichael.com) Impressive museum featuring works by acclaimed indigenous artists and the Group of Seven, Canada's foremost landscape painters.

Aga Khan Museum (77 Wynford Dr, North York; https://agakhanmuseum.org) First North American museum dedicated to Islamic art with a magnificent collection spanning over 1000 years.

Scarborough Bluffs (pictured) Dramatic lakeshore cliffs and cathedral-spire formations good for hiking and birding.

For Kids

COLIN WOODS/SHUTTERSTOCK ©

Toronto is a kid-friendly city with a wide range of options for children of all ages: museums and parks, sights and thrills, even beaches and water play. The city makes it easy for families too – from discounted admission rates to kids-stay-free hotel perks. Add kid menus and restaurants that graciously accommodate picky eaters and you've got a happy little traveler.

Best for Animal Lovers

Ripley's Aquarium of Canada More than 16,000 sea creatures swimming past, around and overhead delight at the aquarium. (pictured; p50)

Riverdale Farm A working urban farm, where children learn about rural life through hands-on fun. (p138)

Spadina Quay Wetlands Explore these wetlands and discover birds, butterflies, turtles...even beavers! (p36)

Best for Creatives

Art Gallery of Ontario Activity stations and a center for DIY art projects keep restless kids happy. (p92)

Harbourfront Centre Watch artists at work – blowing glass, hand-building ceramics, creating textile art. (p30)

Young People's Theatre Catch a play created just for kids. Shows are aimed at different age groups, from under one to over 12s. (p70)

Best for Outdoor Play

High Park Kids enjoy trails, creeks and guided nature walks at this beautiful park. (p118)

Ward's Island Beach A Toronto Islands beach with calm waters and soft tawny sand, perfect for sandcastles. (p41)

Need to Know

Activities Check out www.helpwevegotkids.com for tips on activities, childcare and more.

Transport Kids aged 12 and under ride the TTC for free.

Admission Most sights offer kids free or reduced admission.

LGBTIQ+

To say Toronto is LGBTIQ+ friendly is an understatement. That it embraces diversity more fully than most other cities its size is closer to the mark. In fact, in 2003 Toronto became the first North American city to legalize same-sex marriage. Ground zero of LGBTIQ+ life is the Village, drawing everyone from biker bears to lipstick lesbians to its sunny patios, clubs and cafes.

BOBNOAH/SHUTTERSTOCK ©

Best LGBTIQ+ Nightlife

O'Grady's Irish pub popular for its patio and Dirty Bingo Nights, hosted by drag queens. (pictured; p86)

Crews & Tangos Welcoming bar that doubles as a dance club on weekends. (p87)

Woody's/Sailor Longtime go-to with entertainment and dancing on one side and a sleek bar on the other. (p88)

Glad Day World's oldest gay bookstore, featuring Saturday-night dance parties. (p88)

Best Places to Stay

Anndore House Top choice for style and comfort in the Village. (p148)

Downtown Home Inn Charming B&B with shared bathrooms. (p148)

Victoria's Mansion Inn & Guesthouse Longtime fave of LGBTIQ+ travelers. (p149)

Best LGBTIQ+ Resources

519 (www.the519.org) City agency supporting the LGBTIQ+ community, from recreational classes to counseling.

Canadian Lesbian & Gay Archives (www.clga.ca) Extensive collection of Canadian LGBTIQ+ documentary heritage, open to the public.

Hassle Free Clinic (www.hasslefreeclinic.org) Nonprofit providing free sexual health services, including HIV testing.

Queer West (www.queerwest.org) Up-to-date listings of LGBTIQ+ friendly events, bars and restaurants in the Village and West End.

Four Perfect Days

Day 1

COLIN WOODS/SHUTTERSTOCK ©

First thing, head to the top of the **CN Tower** (p44) for spectacular city views. Walk across the glass floors, if you dare. Afterward, check out **Ripley's Aquarium of Canada** (pictured; p50), where sea creatures swim past visitors in darkened galleries and glass tunnels.

Next, hit **City Hall** (p82) with its clamshell towers and flying-saucer building. Take a photo with the iconic 'Toronto' sign in Nathan Phillips Square.

Walk to Church and Wellesley Sts, the heart of the Village. Pop into gems like **Dead Dog Records** (p89) and **Glad Day** (p88), the world's longest-running gay bookstore. Afterward, play Dirty Bingo at **O'Grady's** (p86), where drag queens call out numbers and hand out risqué prizes.

Day 2

GILBERTO MESQUITA/SHUTTERSTOCK ©

Get an early start at the historic **St Lawrence Market** (p60), selling everything from local produce to fresh bread. Nibble your way through it. On weekends, a **Farmers Market** (p61) and **Antique Market** (p61) set up across the street.

Afterward, explore the **Distillery District** (pictured; p65), a set of Victorian-era factories re-purposed into boutique shops, restaurants and more.

Take Bus 72 to the **Harbourfront Centre** (p30), a collection of waterfront parks, stages and galleries. Visit **Power Plant Contemporary Art Gallery** (p35), showcasing emerging artists. Cross the plaza to the Harbourfront Centre's **main building** (p30) to see what's playing and to take a spin on the **ice rink** (p36).

Day 3

Start at the magnificent **Royal Ontario Museum** (pictured; p104), a massive natural and world history museum. Pick a few sections – Chinese Architecture, First People's Art, Dinosaurs – and call it a morning.

Walk to Kensington Market. Pop into vintage and secondhand stores, keeping an eye out for **Courage My Love** (p100) for clothing and accessories and **Bungalow** (p101) for retro and modern homegoods. Check out the street art – walk down alleys, crane your neck – and consider stopping for a sweet snack at **Dipped Donuts** (p98).

Afterward, catch a set at **Horseshoe Tavern** (p99), an iconic stage for local indie rock, or at **Rex** (p100), an outstanding jazz venue.

Day 4

Start your day at **Tommy Thompson Park** (p72), a birder's paradise. Enjoy the sight of water birds, the glittering lake, and downtown Toronto in the distance.

Take Streetcar 501 on Queen St E to the West End, stepping off near Trinity Bellwoods Park. Spend the afternoon window-shopping at hot-ticket shops like **Type Books** (p128) for off-the-beaten-track reads, **House of Vintage** (p127) for designer wear, and **Craft Ontario Shop** (p127) for art by locals.

After dinner at **Otto's Bierhalle** (p122), walk to **Gladstone Hotel** (pictured; p124) for poetry slams and burlesque or head to **Bar Raval** (p124), a Gaudí-esque spot with strong cocktails and fine wines.

Need to Know

For detailed information, see Survival Guide p147

Currency
Canadian dollar ($)

Time
Eastern Standard Time
(GMT/UTC minus four
hours)

Languages
English, French

Money
The Canadian dollar ($)
is the local currency.
ATMs are widely
available. Credit cards
are accepted in most
hotels and restaurants.

Cell Phones
GSM phones
typically work in
Canada. Arrange for
international coverage
if you don't already
have it.

Tipping
Waitstaff: 15% to 20%
Bartenders: $1 to
$2 per drink or 15%,
depending on locale
Porters: $2 per bag
Housekeepers: from $5
per day
Taxi drivers: 10% to
15%

Daily Budget

Budget: Less than $100
Dorm bed: $30–50
Double room in a hostel or budget hotel: $100–140
Self-catered meals from markets and supermarkets: $8–14
Subway/streetcar/bus fare: $3.25

Midrange: $100–250
Room in a B&B or midrange hotel: $150–250
Meal at a good local restaurant: from $20 plus drinks
Museum/sight admission: $5–20
Short taxi trip: $10–12

Top end: More than $250
Four-star-hotel room: from $250
Three-course meal at a top restaurant:
from $60 plus drinks
Theater tickets: $40–175
Rental car per day: $60–85

Advance Planning

Three months before Buy tickets for a Maple
Leafs game or a big-ticket show at the Princess
of Wales Theatre.

One month before Book your stay, especially
at smaller places such as inns, B&Bs and
hostels.

One week before Check out what festivals
and events are going on when you'll be in town;
make reservations at high-end or happenin'
restaurants.

Arriving in Toronto

✈ **Toronto Pearson International Airport**

Fast rides downtown on UP Express cost $12.35 (kids free); a taxi costs $60.

✈ **Billy Bishop Toronto City Airport**

Quick access via free ferry and pedestrian tunnel; free shuttle to both from Union Station.

🚍 **Union Station**

Direct access to subway (Yellow line), streetcars (6, 72B, 121, 509, 510A), GO commuter buses and trains, and VIA long-distance trains.

🚍 **Toronto Coach Terminal**

Long-distance bus terminal located one block from the Yellow subway line (Dundas).

Getting Around

Ⓢ **Subway**

Fastest way across town; 6am (8am Sunday) to 1:30am.

🚋 **Streetcar**

Extensive service throughout Toronto; 24 hours.

🚌 **Bus**

Best for areas outside Toronto's core; 6am (8am Sunday) to 1am.

⛴ **Boat**

Ferries and water taxis provide access to the Toronto Islands.

🚲 **Bike**

Best for the Waterfront and the Toronto Islands

🚕 **Taxi**

Easily hailed downtown. Metered fares from $4.25, plus $1.75 per kilometer.

Union Station

Toronto Neighborhoods

West End (p117)
Fun to explore, Toronto's ever-popular West End has diverse eateries, posh shopping and trendy bars. Plus the lovely High Park at the far end.

Kensington Market & Chinatown (p91)
A fun, artsy, neighborhood, with used clothing shops, cool little cafes and one of Canada's finest museums – the Art Gallery of Ontario.

◉ Royal Ontario Museum

Art Gallery ◉ of Ontario

◉ High Park

CN Tower

Entertainment & Financial Districts (p43)
Toronto's bustling downtown has loads of must-sees, including the Hockey Hall of Fame, Graffiti Alley and the ultimate skyscraper – the CN Tower.

Waterfront (p29)
Toronto's long waterfront has sunny pathways, leafy parks, a huge arts complex and even a colonial era fort, all with shimmering views of Lake Ontario.

Yorkville & the Annex (p103)
Busy urban strip with luxury shopping on one end, and cheap eats and university bars on the other. Home to several excellent museums.

Downtown Yonge (p75)
Dense and gritty, and home to terrific destinations like the Elgin and Winter Garden Theatre and the Village, Toronto's spirited gay district.

Evergreen Brick Works

Elgin & Winter Garden Theatre

St Lawrence Market Complex

Harbourfront Centre

Tommy Thompson Park

East Toronto & Rosedale (p131)
Once the outskirts of town, East Toronto is popular for its parks and greenways, rich ethnic enclaves, and a fast-rising food and drink scene on Queen Street East.

Toronto Islands

Old Town, Corktown & Distillery District (p59)
Attractive and walkable, this neighborhood's centuries-old complexes have been reborn as popular gathering spots, filled with bars, galleries, farmers markets and more.

Explore
Toronto

St Lawrence Market (p60)
EQROY/SHUTTERSTOCK ©

Explore ◈

Waterfront

It's easy to forget, amid Toronto's bustle and chic urbanity, that the city hugs a huge, gorgeous lake. That makes the Waterfront District all the more delightful, with its lakeside parks, art installations, biking and boating. It's all just a few blocks from the CN Tower, yet it remains a locals' secret, mostly due to the relative lack of hotels and well-known restaurants. But the Waterfront is a worthy escape, especially on one of Toronto's bright spring or summer days.

The Short List

◦ **Harbourfront Centre (p30)** *Exploring galleries, performance venues, boat tours and ice skating, all with beautiful lake views, at this huge outdoor arts and culture complex.*

◦ **Power Plant Contemporary Art Gallery (p35)** *Recharging your contemporary-art batteries at this popular gallery, with its ever-evolving collection and distinctive painted smokestack.*

◦ **Fort York National Historic Site (p36)** *Reliving the War of 1812 with tours of the fort's structures as well as live marching and musket demonstrations.*

◦ **Martin Goodman Trail (p37)** *Biking or strolling along a section of this famous 56km lakefront trail.*

Getting There & Around

🚋 Streetcars 509 and 510 run along Queens Quay W, heading to the West Side and neighborhoods to the north.

🏃 Wide sidewalks and a well-maintained trail make the Waterfront very walkable.

🚗 Avoid driving as parking is very limited.

Neighborhood Map on p34

Martin Goodman Trail (p37) through the Humber Bay Arch Bridge
BILL BROOKS/ALAMY STOCK PHOTO ©: HUMBER BAY ARCH BRIDGE ARCHITECTS, MONTGOMERY & SISAM

Top Experience 📷

Enjoy a free festival at Harbourfront Centre

Practically a neighborhood unto itself, the Harbourfront Centre spreads out over a huge area along the waterfront (4 hectares in all), with an engaging collection of galleries, theaters, places to hang out and paths to stroll down.

◉ MAP P34, D3

✆ 416-973-4000

www.harbourfrontcentre.com

235 Queens Quay W

🕐 10am-11pm Mon-Sat, to 9pm Sun

P 🚻

🚋 509, 510

Events & Festivals

One of the biggest draws of the Harbourfront Centre is its events and festivals, many of them free. In summer, Thursdays mean **Dancing on the Pier**, which brings live bands and locals in dancing shoes (flip-flops included). In winter the Natrel Rink (p36) becomes a disco with rainbow lights on Saturday nights, with a DJ spinning tunes and folks skating to the beats. Concerts are regularly held in the parks and theaters too.

Power Plant Contemporary Art Gallery

The Power Plant (pictured; p35) is a perfect example of repurposing: a 1926 power plant converted into an airy, two-story art gallery with lake views. Year-round it has rich exhibitions of contemporary work by Canadian and international artists. Above all, the gallery aims to reach a diverse audience, doing so by displaying pieces that address current social issues and by showcasing the work of emerging artists. Free admission ensures that the works, and voices, are accessible to all.

Craft & Design Studios

Wander through the main building of the Harbourfront Centre and you'll encounter open art studios, visible from the outside through glass walls. At this incubator and training center **artists-in-residence** work in five areas: glass, ceramics, design, textiles and jewelry. The public is encouraged to watch and engage with the artists to learn about the art forms. Like what you see? Stop by the on-site **Harbourfront Centre Shop** (☏416-973-4993; ◷11am-6pm; 🚋509, 510), which sells works by current and former artists-in-residence.

★ Top Tips

○ Renting a bike is fun way to explore the Harbourfront Centre's offerings; with dedicated bike lanes along the waterfront, it's safe, too.

○ Adirondack chairs are set up along the waterfront – perfect places to have a picnic lunch with a view.

○ Lots of festivals and events are held here year-round. Check the website or stop by the **info desk** to find out what's on.

✗ Take a Break

Don't miss Boxcar Social (p38), a urban-chic cafe in the main building, formerly part of the port complex. It has a terrific patio and lake views to complement its light menu and coffee drinks.

Walking Tour 🥾

Along the Lake

Toronto's waterfront district is just south of the downtown area and CN Tower, yet pleasingly removed from the bustle of the city center. Attractions range from the colonial-era Fort York to the delightful Harbourfront Centre, with its industrial chic cafe, modern art museum and boat tour operators. Enjoy the sunshine and cool lake breezes as you walk between sights.

Walk Facts

Start Fort York National Historical Site

End Queens Quay Terminal

Length 3.2km; 3½ hours

❶ Fort York

Start your tour with a bit of history at the **Fort York National Historic Site** (p36), featuring musket displays and docents in period dress. Exiting the fort area, but staying on the Fort York grounds, follow the footpath to **The Bentway**, an innovative park located underneath the elevated Gardiner Expwy. A figure-eight path is used for ice skating in winter and for strolling and art displays the rest of the year.

❷ Martin Goodman Trail

Exit at the eastern end of The Bentway and walk south through **June Callaway Park**, which runs adjacent to Bastion St, to busy Lakeshore Ave. You'll have to walk a block east to the crosswalk to get across the busy street; afterward, continue south on Stadium St, then turn left onto Queens Quay West. This is a section of the **Martin Goodman Trail** (p37), Ontario's famous lakefront pathway.

❸ Toronto Music Garden

Walking east, in a block you'll pass cozy **Little Norway Park**, near the **entrance to the municipal airport** (p149) – oddly enough. Then, a couple blocks further, the **Toronto Music Garden** (p35), with its Bach-inspired landscaping, and **Spadina Quay Wetlands** (p36), are both on a thin wedge of reclaimed greenery between Queens Quay W and the Spadina Quay Marina.

❹ HTO Waterfront Parks

Continuing east, you'll pass the twin **HTO** urban waterfront parks (the name is a play on H_2O and TO, for Toronto) and three **Wavedecks** – short, playful undulating boardwalks that replaced ugly sections of retaining wall – at Spadina Ave and Rees and Simcoe Sts.

❺ Harbourfront Centre

Ultimately you'll reach the main building of the **Harbourfront Centre** (p30), the Waterfront's crown jewel. Budget plenty of time to explore this large complex. You can grab a coffee or a bite to eat at **Boxcar Social** (p38), ponder modern artwork at the outstanding **Power Plant Contemporary Art Gallery** (p35), perfect your salchow at the **Natrel Rink** (p36) or book a harbor tour – options range from **kayaking** (p37) to **cruises** (📞416-203-0178; www.mariposacruises.com; Queens Quay Terminal, 207 Queens Quay W; 45min tours adult/child $26/20; ⏲May-Sep; ♿; 🚋509, 510).

❻ Queen's Quay Terminal

There's just one more stop after the Harbourfront Centre: **Queen's Quay Terminal** (p39). Built in a repurposed warehouse, and located adjacent to the center, it has a handful of tour operators and eateries on the ground floor.

Waterfront

ST LAWRENCE

Sugar Beach Park

Lower Jarvis St

Jarvis St Slip

St James Park

Adelaide St E

King St E

FINANCIAL DISTRICT

King
Yonge St
Union

Front St E

The Esplanade

Gardiner Expwy

Cooper St

Freeland St

Queens Quay E

Yonge St Slip

Toronto Islands Ferries

Queens Quay

Harbour Square Park

For reviews see
◉ Top Experiences p30
◎ Sights p35
✖ Eating p38
🍷 Drinking p39

500 m
0.25 miles

Toronto Inner Harbour

St Andrew

University Ave

Union Station

Bay St

York St

Harbourfront

Bobbie Rosenfeld Park

Martin Goodman Trail

HARBOURFRONT 13

Harbourfront Centre

York St Slip

Tall Ship Kajama

Power Plant Contemporary Art Gallery

THEATRE BLOCK

Wellington St W

Front St W

Simcoe St

CN Tower

Rogers Centre

Bremner Blvd

Harbourfront Canoe & Kayak Centre

Rees St Slip

Peter St Slip

7

8 10
Wheel Excitement 6
11 1
12
9
Natrel
Simcoe St Rink
Simcoe St Slip

Blue Jays Way

Clarence Square Park

Fort York Blvd Canoe Landing Park

Spadina Ave

Gardiner Expwy

Queens Quay W

Toronto Music Garden

2
3
Spadina Ave Slip
Spadina Quay Wetlands

Billy Bishop Airport Tunnel

King St W

Wellington St W

Front St W

Adelaide St W

Portland St

Bathurst St

Lake Shore Blvd W

Little Norway Park

Western Channel

Billy Bishop Toronto City Airport

Tecumseth St

Niagara St

Fort York National Historic Site

2 4

Exhibition Place (600m)

Sights

Power Plant Contemporary Art Gallery
GALLERY

1 ◎ MAP P34, D3

Easily recognized by its painted smokestack, the Power Plant gallery is just that: a former power plant transformed into Toronto's premier gallery of contemporary art. Best of all, it's free and exhibitions change regularly. Free kid-centered tours and workshops are offered throughout the month; call to reserve a spot. It's part of the Harbourfront Centre (p30) complex. (📞416-973-4949; www.the powerplant.org; 231 Queens Quay W; free; ⏱10am-5pm Tue, Wed & Fri-Sun, to 8pm Thu; 🅿 👫; 🚋509, 510)

Toronto Music Garden
GARDENS

2 ◎ MAP P34, B3

Delicately strung along the western harbor front, the Toronto Music Garden was designed in collaboration with cellist Yo-Yo Ma. It expresses Bach's *Suite No 1 for Unaccompanied Cello* through landscape, with an arc-shaped grove of conifers, a swirling path through a wildflower meadow and a grass-stepped amphitheater where free concerts are held, including **Summer Music in the Garden**, a classical series presented every Thursday (7pm) and Sunday (4pm) from June to September. (📞416-973-4000; www. harbourfrontcentre.com; 479 Queens Quay W; 🚋509, 510)

Toronto Music Garden

Spadina Quay Wetlands

PARK

3 MAP P34, B3

A former lakeside parking lot has been transformed into the 2800-sq-meter Spadina Quay Wetlands, a thriving, sustainable ecosystem full of frogs, birds, fish and butterflies. When lakeside fishers noticed that northern pike were spawning here each spring, the city took it upon itself to create this new habitat. Complete with flowering heath plants, poplar trees and a birdhouse, it's a little gem that led the way in the harborfront's redevelopment. (☏416-392-1111; www.toronto.ca; 479 Queens Quay W; ⏲dawn-dusk; 🚋509, 510)

Fort York National Historic Site

HISTORIC SITE

4 MAP P34, A2

Established by the British in 1793 to defend the then town of York, Fort York was almost entirely destroyed during the War of 1812 when a small band of Ojibwe warriors and British troops were unable to defeat their US attackers. Several structures – barracks, block houses and powder magazines – were immediately rebuilt and still stand on the 17-hectare site. From May to September, men decked out in 19th-century British military uniforms carry out marches and drills, firing musket volleys into the sky. (☏416-392-6907; www.fortyork.ca; 250 Fort York Blvd; adult/child $14/6; ⏲10am-5pm Jun-Aug, 10am-4pm Mon-Fri, to 5pm Sat & Sun Sep-May; 🅿🚻; 🚋509, 511)

Local Experiences 💬

Working out If you're looking for some exercise, skip the hotel gym and go for a jog along the waterfront paths.

Eating Join office workers at **Queen's Quay Terminal** (p39) for a quick or cheap bite.

Working remotely Weekday mornings, **Boxcar Social** (p38) is filled with locals on their laptops.

Sugar Beach Park

BEACH

5 MAP P34, F3

Named after the Redpath Sugar Refinery next door, Sugar Beach is a sweet little spot located near Old Toronto. The urban beach park is filled with pastel-pink umbrellas and located by the water, so you can enjoy scenic views and sandy toes. Swimming is prohibited, unfortunately, but a maple-leaf splash pad kinda makes up for it. (www.toronto.ca; 11 Dockside Dr; free; ⏲8am-11pm; 🚻; 🚋6, 72)

Natrel Rink

ICE SKATING

6 MAP P34, D3

A great little ice rink fronting Lake Ontario that's popular with kids and grown-ups alike. Saturday night brings DJ Skate Nights and a party vibe. Skate rentals (adult/child $13/8) are available, including helmets for kids. (☏416-954-9866; www.harbourfrontcentre.com;

Harbourfront Centre, 235 Queens Quay W; free; ⊙9am-10pm Sun-Thu, to 11pm Fri & Sat Nov-Mar; 🚻; 🚋509, 510)

Martin Goodman Trail   WALKING

7 ◉ MAP P34, C3

The Martin Goodman Trail, a 56km path running the length of Toronto's lakeshore, cuts through the Waterfront neighborhood. The relatively flat path is mostly paved; it's used by joggers, cyclists and folks just out for a stroll. From here, the prettiest direction is east toward the Humber River Bridge, passing urban parks and beaches along the way. (Queens Quay W)

Harbourfront Canoe & Kayak Centre   WATER SPORTS

8 ◉ MAP P34, C3

Centrally located, this outfit makes it easy to get on the water, with kayak, canoe and paddleboard rentals. Two- to three-hour guided tours of the Toronto Islands – in either a kayak or a traditional voyageur canoe – are offered, too. (Paddle Toronto; ☎416-203-2277; https://paddletoronto.com; 283 Queens Quay W; kayaks/canoes/paddleboards for up to 2hr from $45/60/50, tours per person $50-135; ⊙noon-8:30pm Mon-Fri, 10am-5:30pm Sat & Sun; 🚻; 🚋509, 510)

Military re-enactment, Fort York National Historic Site

Tall Ship Kajama

BOATING

9 ◉ MAP P34, D3

The dashing 165ft three-masted *Kajama,* a 1930 German trading schooner, sails from the foot of Lower Simcoe St; there's usually a ticket kiosk beside Queens Quay Terminal. Reservations can be made online. (☎416-203-2322; www.tallshipcruisestoronto.com; 249 Queens Quay W, Suite 111; 90min cruises adult/child $31/17; ☉May-Sep; ♿; 🚋509, 510)

Wheel Excitement

CYCLING

10 ◉ MAP P34, C3

Close to the ferries for the Toronto Islands; day rentals here are cheaper than hiring on Centre Island and give you the freedom to explore further afield. Options include road bikes, cruisers and hybrids. (☎416-260-9000; www.wheelexcitement.ca; 249 Queens Quay W; bicycles per hour/day $15/35; ☉10am-5pm; 🚋509, 510)

Eating

Boxcar Social

CAFE $

11 ✖ MAP P34, D3

An industrial-chic cafe/bar/coffee haven, Boxcar Social has enviable views of Lake Ontario. The menu matches the vibe, with fresh takes on salads and sandwiches (kale caesar salad, anyone?). Mornings bring locals with coffee and computers; evenings bring drinks on the patio and twinkling lights. (☎844-726-9227; www.boxcarsocial.ca; Harbourfront Centre, 235 Queens Quay

Tall Ship Kajama

Canadian National Exhibition

Dating from 1879, '**The Ex**' (CNE; ☎ 416-263-3330; www.theex.com; btwn Strachan Ave & Dufferin St; adult/child $20/16; ⊗late Aug-early Sep; 🚼; 🚋509, 511) features more than 700 exhibitors, agricultural shows, lumberjack competitions, outdoor concerts and carnivalia at **Exhibition Place** (☎416-263-3600; www.explace.on.ca; btwn Strachan Ave & Dufferin St; 🅿; 🚋509, 511), off Lake Shore Blvd W, in the 18 days leading up to Labour Day (the first Monday of September). The air show and Labour Day fireworks take the cake.

W; mains $12-18; ⊗9am-5pm Mon, to 11pm Tue-Thu, to late Fri, 10am-late Sat, to 8pm Sun; 🛜🖉; 🚋509, 510)

Queen's Quay Terminal   FAST FOOD $

12 🔀 MAP P34, D3

A big commercial center right on the water with a lots of fast eats and a couple of chain restaurants. There's a small supermarket inside, too, with a great prepared-food section (there's even sushi made to order!). Good if you're looking to get a quick bite or fixins' for a picnic by the water. (207 Queens Quay W; mains from $5; ⊗7am-10pm Mon-Fri, 8am-10pm Sat & Sun; 🚋509, 510)

Harbour 60   STEAK $$$

13 🔀 MAP P34, D2

Inside the isolated 1917 Toronto Harbour Commission building, this baroque dining room glows with brass lamps and plush booths. Indulge yourself in a variety of enormous steaks, seasonal Florida stone-crab claws and broiled Caribbean lobster tail. Side dishes are big enough for two. Reservations essential. (☎416-777-2111; www.harboursixty.com; 60 Harbour St; mains $20-175; ⊗11:30am-2am Mon-Fri, 5pm-2am Sat, to midnight Sun; 🚋509, 510)

Drinking

Against the Grain Urban Tavern   PUB

14 🚇 MAP P34, F3

The best feature of this yuppyish pub is its enormous lakefront patio (seasonal), with some of the best views of the Toronto harbor front. Come with a friend to enjoy the sunshine and a couple of martinis. If you get hungry, share a plate of sesame-ginger calamari. (☎647-344-1562; http://fabrestaurants.ca/restaurant/against-the-grain-corus-quay; 25 Dockside Dr; ⊗11am-10pm Mon-Thu, to midnight Fri, 10:30am-midnight Sat, to 10pm Sun; 🚋509)

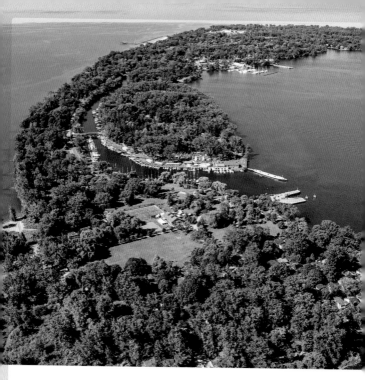

Top Experience 📷
See the city skyline from Toronto Islands

There's no better place to admire Toronto's scenic skyline and enjoy a day of leisure than the Toronto Islands. Just 2km offshore, they offer several rustic beaches and waterways for paddling, all accessible via lakeshore bike paths. Best of all, the islands are car-free. Things definitely get jammed in summer; but indie-minded travelers can still find pockets of true getaway.

www.torontoisland bicyclerental.com

Centre Island

per hour bicycles/ tandems $9/16, 2-/4-seat quadricycles $18/32

🕙 11am-5pm May-Sep

🚩 Centre Island

Skyline Views

The skyline views from the Toronto Islands are, without a doubt, some of the best in the city. Pedal to the north side of the islands for the best photo ops. A favorite spot is just east of the Centre Island ferry dock at **Olympic Island**, where a big grassy field, Adirondack chairs and cityscape views invite a leisurely break.

Ward's Island Beach

A short bike ride from the Ward's Island ferry, this like-named beach is long and curving, with tawny sand. The water is calm – there's barely a wave to be had – due to the proximity of Tommy Thompson Park across the water. (In fact, boaters tend to anchor here.) Popular with locals, it's an especially good getaway from the mainland hubbub.

Hanlan's Point Beach

One of the only clothing-optional beaches in all of Canada, Hanlan's Point Beach is a laid-back spot with gorgeous sunset views. Though it's not required, most people bare all. Located at the western end of the Toronto Islands, a bike trail leads straight there.

Paddling Around the Islands

Join a stand-up paddling tour with **Toronto Island SUP** (☎416-899-1668; www.torontoisland sup.com; 13 Algonquin Bridge Rd, Algonquin Island; 2hr tours from $79, yoga $49, rental 1st hour $30, additional hour $10; ⏱10:30am-before sunset Mon-Fri, 10am-6pm Sat & Sun; 🚢Ward's Island) to explore the 14 islands of the Toronto Islands archipelago. Morning and afternoon excursions focus on flora and fauna, while night tours let you take in the city views. There are whimsical ukulele tours (yep, paddle and play) and yoga classes on the water, too. Cycle to Algonquin Bridge where SUP boarders launch.

★ **Top Tips**

○ The only bike rental on-island is on Centre Island beach, a short walk from the ferry. It's only open in summer.

○ Many people bring bikes from the mainland; rentals are available on the waterfront.

○ During low season most shops are closed and restaurants are open on weekends only.

✗ **Take a Break**

Riviera (☎416-203-2152; www.island riviera.com; 102 Lakeshore Ave, Ward's Island; mains $12-17; ⏱11am-11pm; 🛜🚲; 🚢Ward's Island) is a somewhat upscale restaurant with a terrific tree-shaded patio and lake views.

★ **Getting There**

Ferries to Centre Island and Hanlan's Point (summer only), and Ward's Island (year-round) run from Jack Layton Ferry Terminal frequently and only take 15 minutes.

AD 1885

HOCKEY HALL OF FAME

CLASS OF 2020
IGINLA

CLASS OF 2020
LOWE

CLASS OF
WILS

Explore ◈

Entertainment & Financial Districts

The Entertainment and Financial Districts are Toronto's beating heart, home to Canada's 'Wall St,' Union Station (the country's busiest transportation hub) and the city's best-known attractions and nightlife. City sidewalks are ever busy with businesspeople, students, tourists and street performers. It's a logical place for visitors to start, with the CN Tower, Hockey Hall of Fame, theaters, sports and more nearby.

The Short List

○ *CN Tower (p44)* Enjoying awe-inspiring views from the one-time tallest freestanding tower in the world.

○ *Hockey Hall of Fame (p50)* Practicing your slap shots and admiring the memorabilia at this shrine to Canada's favorite sport.

○ *Performing arts (p56)* Taking in a big-ticket show at any number of impressive theaters, from uber-modern to turn of the last century.

○ *Spectator sports (p57)* Joining local fans to cheer on Toronto's high-flying professional sports teams.

Getting There & Around

Ⓢ The Yellow line has lots of stops downtown that will leave you within a stone's throw of most sights and attractions.

🚋 Numerous streetcar lines converge on downtown, including the 510, heading north–south on Spadina Ave, and east–west routes like the 505 and 506.

Neighborhood Map on p48

Hockey Hall of Fame (p50) ROBERTO MACHADO NOA/SHUTTERSTOCK ©

Top Experience 📷

Walk CN Tower's glass floor, 342m up...if you dare

An iconic sight, designed by John Andrews and once the tallest freestanding structure on the planet (553m), the CN Tower is a must-see. Yes, it's expensive. Yes, there are queues. But once you're up there, oohing and aahing over the spectacular city views, looking down 147 stories through glass floors, or even hanging off the outside of the structure, you'll be glad you came.

◎ MAP P48, E5

La Tour CN

☎ 416-868-6937

www.cntower.ca

301 Front St W

Tower Experience adult/child $38/28

🕗 8:30am-11pm

Ⓢ Union

LookOut-Level Views

A 58-second ride on a glass-fronted elevator leads to perhaps the most spectacular sight in the city: a 360-degree view of Toronto, spread below like a shimmering carpet. Floor-to-ceiling windows make it seem as though you could reach out and touch the skyscrapers. (The windows also make taking photos easier: their darkness adjusts relative to the sunlight.) Come at twilight to see the city transform from day to night, almost magical with its twinkling lights.

Outdoor Sky Terrace Glass Floor

The Outdoor Sky Terrace, 342m high, boasts the CN Tower's original glass floor – the world's first when it was inaugurated in 1994. (There's now another one a level up.) Walking across it, seemingly nothing between your steps and the city streets far below, is surprisingly difficult, even for those with no fear of heights. Don't worry, it won't break – designed to withstand the weight of 35 moose, each floor panel is 6.35cm thick, with four layers of clear tempered glass, plus a layer of air for insulation to keep the room warm.

EdgeWalk

Those with nerves of steel can walk around the 1.5m-wide perimeter of the main pod (pictured), with no windows, no fence, no nothing between you and the city far below. Leaning forward over the tips of your toes is encouraged. (Gulp.) A tether to a metal rail keeps you safe.

★ **Top Tips**

o Get here before 10am to avoid the longest lines, especially during summer and school vacations. (Or spend a little extra for a timed ride up.)

o Buy your tickets online or using the CN Tower app to save 15%.

o Skip the SkyPod observation deck – it can become cramped and stuffy, and really isn't worth the extra cost.

o Stay awhile! Buy a drink and settle in with a book or a deck of cards. With no fixed length of stay and plenty of seating, why not?

✗ **Take a Break**

o On the LookOut observation level, **VUE Bistros** sells pastries and baked goods, plus hot and cold drinks, with floor-to-ceiling window views.

o 360° restaurant has upscale lunch and dinner service on a revolving platform.

Walking Tour 🥾

Architecture & Art

The Entertainment and Financial Districts have some of Toronto's most iconic and popular destinations – namely, the CN Tower and Hockey Hall of Fame. But take a stroll along the busy downtown streets, and you'll encounter museums, pocket parks, and some striking artwork and architecture. Time permitting, catch a concert or even a Blue Jays ball game.

Walk Facts

Start Union Station

End Steam Whistle Brewing

Length 2.8km; 2½ hours

❶ Union Station

Start at **Union Station** (☎416-869-3000; https://torontounion.ca; 140 Bay St; Ⓢ Union, 🚋509, 510), Toronto's main transportation hub and Canada's largest train station. Admire its 22 columns, each 12m tall and weighing 75 tons, before heading into the Great Hall with its vaulted ceiling and provincial flags. Meander through the building, exiting via the southernmost door at Bay St.

❷ Hockey Hall of Fame

Turn left, walking through the tunnel, past the **mural of notable indigenous Canadians**. Take a right at Front St. A block later is the rococo facade of the **Hockey Hall of Fame** (p50), once the Bank of Montreal building but now attached to what's called the Crystal Cathedral, a massive, glass-enclosed commercial center.

❸ Design Exchange

Return to Bay St, turn right and you'll see the **Design Exchange** (p51), a tiny design museum housed in what was the Toronto Stock Exchange. Admire the gleaming art deco doors. Head to King St and take a left. Steps away, a small park holds '**The Pasture**,' Joe Fafard's collection of life-size bronze cows in repose, a stark contrast to the skyscrapers above.

❹ Roy Thomson Hall & Pecault Square

Continue on King St to **Roy Thomson Hall**, the Jello-mold-shaped building, home to the **Toronto Symphony Orchestra** (p56). Wander through adjacent **David Pecault Square**, an urban space with stone benches and, on weekdays, pop-up eateries.

❺ Simcoe Park

Cross Wellington St to **Simcoe Park** and Anish Kapoor's striking '**Mountain**' sculpture, with the CN Tower looming in the background.

❻ Rogers Centre

Cross Front St and take the pedestrian bridge over the train tracks. The **Rogers Centre** (p51), home of the Blue Jays, is on the right, the CN Tower on the left. As you walk, admire '**The Audience**,' a baseball-themed frieze by Michael Snow.

❼ CN Tower and Ripley's Aquarium

At the end of the bridge, turn left toward the **CN Tower** (p44) and **Ripley's Aquarium of Canada** (p50). Find the perfect angle to take some selfies with the 553m tower looming above you. Consider heading to the top to enjoy the view.

A · B · C · D

1

Carr St

Wolseley St

Ace La

Bathurst St

Ryerson Ave

Denison Ave

Augusta Ave

Vanauley St

Cameron St

QUEEN
WEST

Sullivan St

Phoebe St

Huron St

Bulwer St

Soho St

Beverley St

Queen St W

2

27 · 28

4 Graffiti
Alley

Richmond St W

Maud St

Camden St

Spadina Ave

3 · 26

401
Richmond

7

24

16
15

11

8

Morrison St

Brant St

Adelaide St W

King St W

Oxley St

Charlotte St

Peter St

Widmer St

19

3

14
12

Thompson
Toronto

Douro St

Brant Pl

Portland St

Draper St

Wellington St W

Clarence
Square
Park

18

Mercer St

Blue Jays Way

Windsor St

Niagara St

4

Front St W

5

Fort York Blvd

Canoe
Landing
Park

Spadina Ave

6
Rogers
Centre

Bremner Blvd

Lake Shore Blvd W

Gardiner Expwy

Bathurst St

Lake Shore Blvd W

6

Queens Quay W

Spadina
Ave
Slip

Peter St
Slip

Rees
St
Slip

A · B · C · D

Entertainment & Financial Districts

Grange Park

Stephanie St

Renfrew Pl Pullan Pl Osgoode Queen St W

Queen

ENTERTAINMENT DISTRICT

17

22

9

29

13

Temperance St

Nelson St

20

Adelaide St W

10

Pearl St

THEATRE BLOCK

21 St Andrew King St W

King

David Pecault Sq 23

Emily St

Design Exchange 5

Wellington St W

FINANCIAL DISTRICT

Piper St

Hockey Hall of Fame 1

Simcoe Park

Union

Front St W

Metro Convention Centre

Station St

Union Station

Ontario Travel Information Centre

CN Tower 2

Ripley's Aquarium of Canada

Bremner Blvd

25

Bobbie Rosenfeld Park

Gardiner Expwy

Harbour St

HARBOURFRONT

Queens Quay W

Simcoe St Slip

York St Slip

McCaul St · St Patrick St · Simcoe St · Bay St · James St · University Ave · York St · Bay St · Yonge St · Duncan St · John St · Simcoe St · John St · York St · Lower Simcoe St · Rees St

0 500 m
0 0.25 miles

For reviews see
◉	Top Experiences	p44
◎	Sights	p50
✕	Eating	p51
◪	Drinking	p54
✪	Entertainment	p55
⌂	Shopping	p57

Sights

Hockey Hall of Fame
MUSEUM

1 ⊙ MAP P48, H4

Inside the rococo gray-stone Bank of Montreal building (c 1885), the Hockey Hall of Fame is a Canadian institution. Even those unfamiliar with the rough, super-fast sport are likely to be impressed by this, the world's largest collection of hockey memorabilia. Check out the *Texas Chainsaw Massacre*–like goalkeeping masks or go head to head with the great Wayne Gretzky, virtual-reality style. And, of course, be sure to take a pic with the beloved Stanley Cup. (☑ 416-360-7765; www.hhof.com; Brookfield Place, 30 Yonge St; adult/child $20/14; ☺ 9:30am-6pm Mon-Sat, 10am-6pm Sun Jun-Sep, 10am-5pm Mon-Fri, 9:30am-6pm Sat, 10:30am-5pm Sun Oct-May; 🚻; Ⓢ Union)

Ripley's Aquarium of Canada
AQUARIUM

2 ⊙ MAP P48, E5

Arguably one of Toronto's best attractions for both young and old, with more than 16,000 aquatic animals and 5.7 million liters of water in the combined tanks. There are touch tanks, a glass tunnel with a moving walkway, educational dive presentations...and even live jazz on the second Friday of each month. Open 365 days a year. Peak hours are 11am to 4pm. (☑ 647-351-3474; www.ripleysaquariumofcanada.

com; 288 Bremner Blvd; adult/child $32/22; ☺ 9am-11pm; 🚻; Ⓢ Union)

401 Richmond
GALLERY

3 ⊙ MAP P48, C2

Inside an early-20th-century lithographer's warehouse, restored in 1994, this 18,500-sq-meter New York–style artists collective hums with the creative vibes of more than 140 contemporary galleries, exhibition spaces, studios and shops representing works in almost any medium you can think of. Speaker series and film fests are held throughout the year. Grab a snack at the ground-floor cafe (open 9am to 5pm Monday to Friday) and enjoy it on the expansive roof garden, a little-known oasis in summer. (☑ 416-595-5900; www.401richmond.com; 401 Richmond St W; free; ☺ 9am-7pm Mon-Fri, to 6pm Sat; 🚋 510)

Graffiti Alley
PUBLIC ART

4 ⊙ MAP P48, B2

Possibly the most popular place to check out street art in Toronto (and there are many), this back alley has a magnificent collection of colorful murals and street art. Spanning three blocks (about 400m), the alley was popularized as the location of Rick Mercer's rants on CBC comedy program the *Rick Mercer Report*. Great for photo ops. (Rush Lane; Graffiti Alley, btwn Spadina Ave & Portland St; 🚋 301, 501)

Design Exchange
MUSEUM

5 ◉ MAP P48, G3

The original Toronto Stock Exchange now houses eye-catching industrial-design exhibits. The permanent collection of this rather tiny museum includes more than 1000 Canadian pieces that span six decades. There are free one-hour tours the last Friday of each month, starting at noon. (DX; 📞416-363-6121; www.dx.org; 234 Bay St; free; 🕑9am-5pm Tue-Fri, noon-4:30pm Sat; S King)

Rogers Centre
STADIUM

6 ◉ MAP P48, D5

Technically awe-inspiring, the Rogers Centre opened in 1989 with the world's first fully retractable dome roof and seating for up to 53,500 people. Tours include a brain-scrambling video wall screening footage of past sporting glories, concerts and events; a sprint through a box suite; a locker-room detour (sans athletes); and a memorabilia museum. A budget seat at a **Blue Jays** (www.bluejays.com) baseball game is the cheapest way to see the center. (📞416-341-2770; 1 Blue Jays Way; 1hr tours adult/child $17/10; S Union)

Eating

Ravi Soups
INTERNATIONAL $

7 🍴 MAP P48, D2

This one's pretty simple: a small menu of seven soups (the likes of corn chowder with blue crab or porcini-mushroom wild-rice bisque), five wraps (eg curried

Ripley's Aquarium of Canada

lamb with roasted yams) and four salads (eg baby spinach with mango-pineapple salsa) that are done to perfection. There's a small eating area with a long shared table and a small patio with psychedelic art. (☎647-435-8365; www. ravisoup.com; 322 Adelaide St W; soups $10.99; ⏱11am-10pm; ☐504, 508)

Wilbur Mexicana
MEXICAN $

8 ❌ MAP P48, B3

This is Mexican street-food heaven, from the industrial-chic atmosphere to the standout Baja fish tacos. Complete with a fully stocked apothecary cabinet filled with salsas and hot sauces, this hip little taco joint pays homage to Wilbur Scoville, founder of the Scoville scale, which measures the spiciness of chilies. (☎416-792-1878; http://wilburmexicana.com; 552 King St W; tacos $4-5, mains $11-15; ⏱11:30am-10pm Mon-Sat, noon-9pm Sun; ☑; ☐504)

Assembly Chef's Hall
FOOD HALL $$

9 ❌ MAP P48, G2

Home to a diverse set of global cuisines by some of Toronto's top chefs, this is less food court and more sprawling upscale eatery. There's everything from margherita pizza to pork *carnitas* tacos and *khao soi* beef. Weekday lunch hours are crowded with suits and professional attire (it's in the heart of the Financial District), but

Union Summer

dinnertime is much more chill and relaxed. (☎647-557-5993; www. assemblychefshall.com; 111 Richmond St E; mains $12-19; ⏱7am-10pm Mon-Fri, 10am-10pm Sat; ☑; Ⓢ Osgoode)

Pai
THAI $$

10 ❌ MAP P48, E3

Pai is known for its spectacular food and lively ambience, so you'll pretty much always see lines out the door no matter the time of day. The *khao soi* (curry noodle soup) is what you might see all over social media; it's definitely one of the best Thai dishes you'll find in town. (☎416-901-4724; www.paitoronto. com; 18 Duncan St; mains $14-18; ⏱11:30am-10pm Mon-Thu, to 10:30pm Fri & Sat, 3-10pm Sun; Ⓢ St Andrew)

Buca

ITALIAN $$$

11 MAP P48, A3

A breathtaking basement-level restaurant with exposed-brick walls and a soaring ceiling, Buca serves artisanal Italian fare such as homemade pasta and nose-to-tail-style dishes such as *orecchio di maiale* (crispy pigs' ears) and *cervello* (lamb's brains wrapped in prosciutto and sage). Ease into the experience with a charcuterie board of house-cured meats, flavorful cheeses and bread knots. (416-865-1600; www.buca.ca; 604 King St W; mains $17-55; 11am-3pm & 5-10pm Mon-Wed, 11am-3pm & 5-11pm Thu & Fri, 5-11pm Sat, 5-10pm Sun; 304, 504)

Lee

ASIAN $$$

12 MAP P48, A3

Truly a feast for the senses, dinner at acclaimed *cuisinier* Susur Lee's self-titled flagship is an experience best shared. Slick servers assist in navigating the artisanal selection of East-meets-West delights: you really want to get the pairings right. It's impossible to adequately convey the dance of flavors, textures and aromas one experiences in the signature Singaporean slaw, with...how many ingredients?! (416-504-7867; www.susur.com/lee; 601 King St W; mains $16-38; 5-10:30pm Sun-Wed, to 11pm Thu, to 11:30pm Fri & Sat; ; 504, 508)

Union Summer

Union Station's daily summer food market – known as **Union Summer** (416-338-0889; http://torontounion.ca; Union Station, 65 Front St W; 11am-9pm Mon-Wed, to 10pm Thu-Sat, to 6pm Sun; ; S Union) – has become a fixture in Toronto, with gourmet food stalls, activities, free outdoor film screenings, live music and drinks from late May to early August.

Richmond Station

INTERNATIONAL $$$

13 MAP P48, H2

Reservations are strongly advised (to avoid disappointment) at this justifiably popular, busy and uncomplicated restaurant, which is the brainchild of celebrity *Top Chef Canada* winner Carl Heinrich. Dishes are 'ingredient focused and technique driven.' Try a delicious charcuterie board and buttery lobster spaghetti. The eclectic menu is simple but gratifying, priced right and complemented by a well-paired wine list and daily chalkboard specials. Highly recommended. (647-748-1444; www.richmondstation.ca; 1 Richmond St W; mains $23-32; 11:30am-10:30pm; S Queen)

Local Experiences

Hanging out

The swanky rooftop lounge at the **Thompson Toronto** (Map p48, A3; 📞 416-640-7778; www.thompsonhotels.com/toronto; 550 Wellington St W; 🅿 ❄ 🛜 ♿ 🐾; 🚊 504, 508) is a go-to for locals year-round – martinis, couches and skyline views; what could top that? During the **Toronto International Film Festival** (p114), celebrities often join in the fun.

Shopping

Sure, souvenir gifts are at all the major downtown sights. But consider heading west to places like **Outer Layer** (p57) and **Spacing Store** (p57), where locals shop for more imaginative gifts and mementos.

Navigation

Head underground: use the city's PATH tunnels to get from place to place and avoid the cold or the traffic.

Forno Cultura
BAKERY

14 🍴 MAP P48, A3

An Italian bakery tucked into a basement-level shop, Forno Cultura offers a full line of bread and pastries made with ingredients imported from Italy – even the flour and butter! The bakery itself is a long room, one side lined with impossible-to-resist goods, the other a view of bakers doing their thing. Communal tables encourage you to stay, watch and eat. (📞416-603-8305; www.fornocultura.com; 609 King St W; items from $3; ⏰7:30am-9:30pm Tue-Sat, 8am-6pm Sun; ✒🧍; 🚊504, 508)

Drinking

Jimmy's
COFFEE

15 ☕ MAP P48, A3

Located in a bohemian-chic row house, this hopping coffee joint serves up flavorful coffee drinks – even nitro cold brew on tap – made from beans roasted in-house. Explore and find a cozy spot: upstairs, downstairs, front patio or back, there are lots of options here. If there's a long line, try the original Jimmy's across the street; same coffee, different vibe. (📞647-347-5600; www.jimmyscoffee.ca; 100 Portland St; ⏰8am-8pm Sun-Thu, to 9pm Fri & Sat; 🚊)

Petty Cash   BAR

16 🚇 MAP P48, A2

This King West hangout is a millennial's favorite known for its killer cocktails and comfort food. Edgy murals and neon signs make it easy to prove you had a good time with an Instagram photo or two. (📞 647-748-2274; http://pettycash toronto.com; 487 Adelaide St W; ⏱ 5pm-2am Mon-Fri, 4pm-2am Sat & Sun; 🚋 504)

Fifth Social Club   CLUB

17 🚇 MAP P48, E2

Known by regulars as Easy, this upscale club hosts an early to mid-20s crowd. From the chocolate-fondue station to the life-size Jenga and the swing in the middle of the dance floor, this is not your ordinary spot for a weekend outing, but if you're looking to dress up and dance the night away, it's perfect. (📞 416-979-3000; http://fifthsocial club.thefifth.com; 225 Richmond St W; cover $20-25; ⏱ 9pm-2:30am Fri, 10pm-2:30am Sat; Ⓢ Osgoode)

Underground Garage   BAR

18 🚇 MAP P48, D3

Trying valiantly to keep it real in a grungy sort of way, this urban rock bar is down a steep staircase lined with Led Zeppelin, Willie Nelson and John Lennon posters. Once inside, it's all about wailing guitars, cold beer and good times (and loads of Christmas lights).

In summer, head to the rooftop patio – same vibe with spectacular views. (📞 416-688-8787; www. undergroundgarage.ca; 365 King St W; cover $8-20; ⏱ 10pm-2am Sun-Wed, 9pm-2am Thu-Sat; 🚋 504, 510)

Entertainment

TIFF Bell Lightbox   CINEMA

19 ⭐ MAP P48, D3

Headquarters of the Toronto International Film Festival (p114), this resplendent cinema complex is the hub of all the action when the festival's in town. Throughout the year it's used primarily for TIFF Cinematheque, screening world cinema, independent films, directorial retrospectives and other special events. Try to see a film here if you can. (📞 888-599-8433; www.tiff.net; 350 King St W; 🚋 504)

Adelaide Hall   CONCERT VENUE

20 ⭐ MAP P48, E2

One of the best small venues in town – its acoustics are tops – Adelaide Hall attracts both big-name and up-and-coming acts. On other nights, DJs and cover bands keep the place hopping. Look for the entrance tucked into an alley off Adelaide St (or just follow the line of people). (📞 647-344-1234; https://adelaidehallto. com; 250 Adelaide St W; 🚇 141, 143, 144, 145)

Roy Thomson Hall, home to the TSO

pipes for over 50 years. Tickets sell out fast, though standing-room-only tickets are available on performance days. Free concerts in the impressive glass-enclosed Richard Bradshaw Amphitheatre are held from September through May, usually at noon. (☑416-363-8231; www.coc.ca; Four Seasons Centre for the Performing Arts, 145 Queen St W; ☉box office 11am-7pm Mon-Sat, to 3pm Sun; Ⓢ Osgoode)

CPAULFELL/SHUTTERSTOCK © ROY THOMSON HALL, ARCHITECT ARTHUR ERICKSON

Royal Alexandra Theatre
THEATER

21 ⭐ MAP P48, F3

The 'Royal Alex,' as she is some-times known, is one of the more im-pressive theaters in town and home to splashy Broadway musicals. Built in 1907, it's among the oldest continuously operating theaters in Canada, its stage graced by some of the most talented 20th-century artists, including Orson Welles, Fred and Adele Astaire and Edith Piaf. (☑416-872-1212; www.mirvish.com; 260 King St W; Ⓢ St Andrew, 🚋504)

Canadian Opera Company
OPERA

22 ⭐ MAP P48, F2

Canada's national opera company has been warbling its phenomenal

Toronto Symphony Orchestra
CLASSICAL MUSIC

23 ⭐ MAP P48, F3

A range of classics, Cole Porter–era pops and new music from around the world are presented by the TSO at Jello-mold-like Roy Thomson Hall (sometimes also at Massey Hall and the Meridian Arts Centre). Reduced ticket prices available (from $19) for music-lovers aged 15 to 35, too. (TSO; ☑416-593-1285; www.tso.ca; Roy Thomson Hall, 60 Simcoe St; ☉box office 10am-5pm Mon-Fri, noon-5pm Sat; Ⓢ St Andrew)

Factory Theatre
THEATER

24 ⭐ MAP P48, A2

This innovative theater company – 'Home of the Canadian Playwright' – has been busy since 1970 pro-ducing exclusively Canadian plays. Stay for the talk backs ('Matt's Chats') with cast members after most shows. Sunday matinees are 'Pay What You Can.' (☑416-504-9971; www.factorytheatre.ca; 125 Bathurst St; tickets from $25; 🚋501, 504A, 504B)

Discounted Show Tickets

Performing-arts tickets aren't cheap in this town, often running $100 or more. Save a few loonies by trying for rush tickets, sold on performance day. For those aged under 30, many venues offer discounted tickets costing just $25.

Scotiabank Arena

SPECTATOR SPORT

25 ⭐ MAP P48, G5

The Scotiabank Arena is home to the 13-time Stanley Cup–winning **Toronto Maple Leafs** (www.mapleleafs.com) and the **Toronto Raptors** (www.nba.com/raptors), the only Canadian team in the NBA. It also hosts countless concerts and big-ticket events. (📞416-815-5500; www.scotiabank arena.com; 40 Bay St; Ⓢ Union)

Shopping

Spacing Store

GIFTS & SOUVENIRS

26 🏠 MAP P48, D2

Spacing is a magazine with a thing for Canadian cities. Its store is a celebration of urban living, with T-shirts, vintage TTC posters and other gifts by local designers. Proudly wear your favorite neighborhood as a button and get the inside staff gossip about upcoming changes to Toronto's streets. (📞416-644-1017; http://spacing.ca/ toronto; 401 Richmond St W; 🕐11am-7pm Mon-Fri, noon-6pm Sat; Ⓢ Osgoode)

Outer Layer

GIFTS & SOUVENIRS

27 🏠 MAP P48, B2

A little gift shop selling whimsical and laugh-out-loud knickknacks, accessories and greeting cards, many with a Torontonian or Canadian spin. It's amazingly well curated – few lame ducks here. (📞416-869-9889; https://outerlayer. com; 577 Queen St W; 🕐11am-7pm Mon-Wed & Sat, to 8pm Thu & Fri, noon-6pm Sun; 🚋 301, 501)

Freshly Baked Tees

CLOTHING

28 🏠 MAP P48, B2

DIY souvenir T-shirt: bring your own text and graphics or have the cool cats behind the desk do it. Ready in five minutes. High-quality cotton T-shirts start at $29. Discounts available for orders of four or more. (📞416-907-3575; 557 Queen St W; 🕐noon-7pm; 🚋 301, 501)

Ben McNally

BOOKS

29 🏠 MAP P48, G2

An independent bookstore owned and run by friendly bookworms, Ben McNally has a wide, interesting selection of titles often not found elsewhere. Book talks and readings are regularly held; check the website for the schedule. (📞416-361-0032; https://benmc nallybooks.com; 366 Bay St; 🕐9am-6pm Mon-Fri, 11am-5pm Sat; 🚌141, 142, 143, 144, 145)

Explore ◈
Old Town, Corktown & Distillery District

This centuries-old part of town has beautifully restored buildings and cobblestone sidewalks, providing a snapshot of Toronto's history. Inside, modern-day fancies take over – bars, upscale eateries, boutique shops and performing-arts spaces. Wander the streets and explore. The ghosts of Toronto's past are here, but the neighborhood is very much alive.

The Short List

○ **St Lawrence Market Complex (p60)** *Perusing fruits, meats and cheeses, plus antiques, curios and even a museum, at this lively marketplace.*

○ **Distillery District (p65)** *Exploring this converted 19th-century distillery, home to a rich array of shops, restaurants and galleries.*

○ **Reservoir Lounge (p69)** *Listening to jazz, blues and swing in an iconic underground joint.*

○ **Chef's House (p67)** *Enjoying a gourmet meal on a food-court budget, prepared by culinary students.*

Getting There & Around

S The yellow line stops near St Lawrence Market at Union Station and King St (at Yonge St).

🚋 Streetcars 503 and 504 run along King St, from the Entertainment & Financial Districts and the East Side.

🚌 Route 121 serves the neighborhood from the Waterfront and Entertainment & Financial Districts.

Neighborhood Map on p64

Flatiron Building (p65) COLIN WOODS/SHUTTERSTOCK ©

Top Experience 📷

Graze the food stalls of St Lawrence Market Complex

A marketplace for over 150 years, the St Lawrence complex is alive with hustle and bustle: food stalls and specialty shops, antique and farmers markets, and the well-restored meeting place St Lawrence Hall, its copper clock tower visible from blocks away. It's a place to explore and enjoy; a place to imagine what life was once like here.

◎ MAP P64, B3

📞 416-392-7219

www.stlawrencemarket.com

92-95 Front St E

🕐 8am-6pm Tue-Thu, to 7pm Fri, 5am-5pm Sat

🅿

🚋 503, 504

Saturday Farmers Market

A cornucopia of colors and flavors greets you at the St Lawrence farmers market. Held every Saturday, it's a bustling affair, bringing locals in to buy fresh produce, artisanal foods and flowers from around the region. Come early – it opens at 5am – for the best of the lot and great photo ops, too. In summer the market spills onto the surrounding streets.

Sunday Antique Market

Over 90 vendors, some from as far as Québec, come to sell their treasures every Sunday at the St Lawrence antique market (pictured). It's an experience: rows and rows of stands filled with everything from books and tableware to jewelry and chandeliers. Considered the best antique market in the city, this is the place to come for a special find or even just a quirky bauble.

Market Kitchen

Located on the mezzanine level of St Lawrence Market South, this 'kitchen' serves as a culinary workshop and event space. One-off classes often include shopping in the market below, meeting vendors and cooking up a feast under the guidance of a professional chef. Others include simply watching the chef prepare a gourmet meal and enjoying it on-site. Either way, it's a win. Ontario wines and craft beers are typically paired with the menus.

Market Gallery

The Market Gallery is a tiny museum with rotating exhibits of paintings, photographs, documents and historical relics of Toronto. It's located at St Lawrence Market South in what was the council chamber – all that remains of Toronto's first City Hall, which stood here from 1845 to 1899. Open Tuesday to Saturday; admission is $8/5 adult/child.

★ Top Tips

○ Browse, sample and snack at several food stalls instead of having a full meal at one place.

○ You'll get the best produce if you arrive first thing in the morning for the Saturday farmers market.

○ Take a cooking class or book a special dinner at the Market Kitchen.

✕ Take a Break

For gourmet dining at St Lawrence Market prices, try Chef's House (p67), where culinary students whip up prix-fixe two-, three- and four-course meals.

Head to the 1950s-style Patrician Grill (p66) for irresistible (and belt-busting) eats such as triple-decker sandwiches and chocolate milkshakes.

Walking Tour 🥾

Old York Meets New

Old meets new in this unique district. Structures that date from the city's founding and industrial hey day also serve as popular destinations for locals and tourists alike. Check out the historic Flatiron Building, adorned with a striking modern mural, and then peruse the farmers market at St Lawrence Market or window-shop in the Distillery District.

Walk Facts
Start Flatiron Building
End Mill Street Brewery
Length 2.7km; three hours

❶ Flatiron Building

Begin at the **Flatiron Building** (p65), the 1892 Gooderham and Worts Distillery headquarters, so named because of its triangular shape. Admire its copper roof and turret as you walk around it, not missing the whimsical **mural** that makes it seem that a curtain of windows is falling off. Head east on Front St. About a block away, stop and turn around for an iconic view: the Flatiron Building perfectly framed by Toronto's skyscrapers.

❷ St Lawrence Market South

Continue east on Front to **St Lawrence Market South** (p60), built in 1845 to serve as Toronto's City Hall. Inside you'll find more than 120 vendors, selling everything from pork belly to raw honey. Wander and graze, taking in the sights and tastes, and check out the **Market Gallery**, with historical exhibits on the city.

❸ Farmers & Antique Markets

Afterward, return to Front St, taking an immediate right down Jarvis St to The Esplanade. On the corner is a huge semi-permanent tent, the temporary home of the **Saturday farmers market** and **Sunday antique market** while the North Market building is reconstructed. Inside, wander past rows upon rows of fresh local produce or, alternatively, antique furniture, tableware and knickknacks.

❹ St Lawrence Hall

Return to Jarvis St, heading north to King St, where **St Lawrence Hall** (p60) sits. A 19th-century meeting place with an impressive copper clock tower, this was where abolitionists campaigned to end slavery in Canada.

❺ Along the Way

Turn right onto King, walking several blocks to Trinity St, along the way poking your head into the **Patrician Grill** (p66) to admire its immaculately preserved 1950s-style diner (if the meat-loaf special is available, be sure to stay and enjoy!). At Trinity St, take a right and continue to Mill St, the heart of the **Distillery District** (p65).

❻ Distillery District

Once the site of the British Empire's largest whiskey distillery, today it's a pedestrian-only area (p65) with cobblestone streets, its factories repurposed into boutiques, galleries, art studios, restaurants and bars. Pop into locally owned **Hoi Bo** (p70) or **Corktown Designs** (p71), or see what's on at the **Young Centre for the Performing Arts** (☎416-866-8666; www.youngcentre.ca; 50 Tank House Lane; ☒72, ☒503, 504). Top off your long walk with a flight at the **Mill Street Brewery** (p68).

Old Town, Corktown & Distillery District

For reviews see

◎	Top Experiences	p60
◉	Sights	p65
⊗	Eating	p66
🍺	Drinking	p68
⊗	Entertainment	p69
⊗	Shopping	p70

0 — 400 m
0 — 0.2 miles

CORKTOWN

DISTILLERY DISTRICT

ST LAWRENCE

St Lawrence Market Complex

Toronto's First Post Office

Moss Park

St James Park

Flatiron Building

Sights

Distillery District AREA

1 ◉ MAP P64, F4

Centered on the 1832 Gooderham and Worts distillery – once
the British Empire's largest – the
5-hectare Distillery District is
one of Toronto's best downtown
attractions. Its Victorian industrial
warehouses have been converted
into soaring galleries, artists studios, design boutiques, cafes and
eateries. On weekends, newlyweds
pose before a backdrop of red brick
and cobblestone, young families
walk their dogs and the fashionable
shop for art beneath charmingly
decrepit gables and gantries. In
summer, expect live jazz, activities,
exhibitions and foodie events.

(☎ 416-364-1177; www.thedistillery
district.com; 9 Trinity St; ⊙10am-7pm
Mon-Wed, to 8pm Thu-Sat, 11am-6pm
Sun; 🚌72, 🚋503, 504)

Flatiron Building HISTORIC BUILDING

2 ◉ MAP P64, B3

An iconic sight in the heart of the
old town, the Flatiron is impossible
to miss. Built in 1892, it's a five-
story iron-shaped building with a
steep copper roof and turret; in the
background, Toronto's skyscrapers provide a beautiful contrast. Be
sure to check out the mural on the
building's western side; created by
Canadian artist Derek Michael Be-
sant, it integrates with the existing
structure to make it appear that a
curtain of windows has not been
properly tacked up.

Distillery District

A long time office building, the Flatiron was originally built for the Gooderham and Worts Distillery's administrative offices (notably, its repurposed factory serves as the central building of the Distillery District; p65). (Gooderham Building; 49 Wellington St E; 🚋503)

Toronto's First Post Office
HISTORIC SITE

3 ◎ MAP P64, A2

Dating from 1834, this national historic site is also the city's oldest surviving post office. A small museum showcases the beginning of the city's postal service back when it was part of the British Royal Mail; the highlight for many is writing a letter with a quill – tougher than it looks! – and posting it. (🕿416-865-1833; https://townofyork.com; 31 Adelaide St E; free; ⊙9am-5:30pm Mon-Fri, 10am-4pm Sat, noon-4pm Sun; 👪; Ⓢ Queen)

Eating

Patrician Grill
DINER $

4 🍴 MAP P64, C3

Built in the 1950s, the Patrician has been run by the same family since 1967. Photographers will have a field day with the neon outside and the original decor inside. Food centers on burgers, BLTs, bacon and eggs (cooked to perfection) and home fries. Friday-lunchtime meat loaf is a local institution and

Global Eats in Old York

There's an almost comical variety of cuisines in this compact area of the city: Japanese, German, Indian, Moroccan, a joint that sells a hundred raw oysters for a hundred bucks, a famous-for-its-Friday-meat-loaf place, even a restaurant run for and by culinary students. The list goes on, and the majority are reasonably priced and conveniently located.

sells out quickly. (🕿416-366-4841; http://patriciangrill.com; 219 King St E; meals $5-16; ⊙7am-4pm Mon-Fri, 8am-2pm Sat; Ⓢ King)

Schnitzel Queen
EUROPEAN $

5 🍴 MAP P64, C1

This poky German takeout specializes in golden-delicious breaded-schnitzel sandwiches that make great picnic fodder. These mammoth creations are excellent value and usually good for two meals – the schnitzel is double the size of the bun. Purists should nab a bar stool and stay in for the authentic dinner plates with mushroom sauce, potato salad and sauerkraut ($11 to $16). (🕿416-504-1311; www.schnitzelqueen.ca; 211 Queen St E; schnitzels $8-12; ⊙11am-9pm Wed, to 10pm Thu & Fri, noon-8pm Sat; 🚋301, 501, 502)

WORKS Gourmet Burger Bistro

BURGERS $$

6 MAP P64, B3

Everything and anything you could ever want in a burger. All burgers at the Works are completely customizable, including the patty, bun, toppings and sides. There are also more than 50 drool-worthy set options if you'd rather have the choice made for you. (☏416-594-9675; https://worksburger.com; 60 Wellington St E; mains $13-19; ⏲11am-10pm Sun-Wed, to 11pm Thu-Sat; Ⓢ King)

Chef's House

CANADIAN $$

7 MAP P64, C3

Enjoy gourmet fare created and served by culinary students at George Brown College. The dining room is upscale and modern, with an open kitchen (see the team hard at work!). The prix-fixe menu changes regularly, but expect delights like citrus-cured salmon, handmade fettuccine with saffron cream and cardamom crème brûlée. An excellent way to eat well on a tight budget. (☏416-415-2260; www.thechefshouse.com; 215 King St E; 2/3/4 courses from $20/25/41; ⏲11:30am-1pm & 6:30-8:30pm Mon-Fri; Ⓢ King)

Pearl Diver

SEAFOOD $$

8 MAP P64, B2

A small, bustling restaurant, this place is known for its regular seafood specials. Come on Thursday for its crowning glory, the '100 for 100': $100 for 100 raw oysters, quickly and expertly shucked

Feather pen, Toronto's First Post Office

Old Town, Corktown & Distillery District Eating

Local Experiences

Art The best time to talk to local artists and check out their **Distillery District studios** (p65) is in the early afternoon – many will have their doors open or signs inviting visitors in.

Eating Join a cooking class or workshop at the **Market Kitchen** (p61), popular with foodies.

Drinking The office crowd packs the house at **Triple A Bar** (p69) most weeknights during happy hour.

(no bits of sand here). On weekends, the lobster benny is where it's at. (📞416-366-7827; https://pearldiver.to; 100 Adelaide St E; mains $16-44; ⏱4pm-midnight Tue & Wed, 11am-1am Thu-Sat, to midnight Sun; 🚋141, 143, 144, 145)

Nami JAPANESE $$

9 🚇 MAP P64, A2

Nami, meaning 'wave' (as in tsunami), is unmissable for its cool blue-neon wave on the outside of the building. Bustling about the black-lacquered interior are kimono-clad hostesses and intense sushi chefs, who make only small concessions to North American palates. *Robatayaki* grilling is a specialty, so this is *the* place to try home-style *sukiyaki* hot pot. (📞416-362-7373; www.namirestaurant.

ca; 55 Adelaide St E; lunch sets $18-24, dinner mains from $28, sukiyaki per person $48; ⏱11:45am-2pm & 5:30-10pm Mon-Fri, 5:30-10pm Sat; 🚇King)

Drinking

Mill Street Brewery BREWERY

10 🚇 MAP P64, F4

With 13 specialty beers made on-site in the atmospheric Distillery District (p65), these guys are a leading light in local microbrewing. Order a sample platter so you can taste all the award-winning brews, including the Tankhouse Pale Ale, Stock Ale and Organic Lager. On a sunny afternoon the courtyard is the place to be. The beer-friendly food includes burgers and wraps. (📞416-681-0338; www.millstreet brewery.com; 21 Tank House Lane; ⏱11am-1am Sun-Wed, to 2am Thu-Sat; 🚋72, 🚋503, 504)

C'est What PUB

11 🚇 MAP P64, B3

More than 30 whiskeys and six dozen Canadian microbrews (mostly from Ontario) are on hand at this underground pub (look for a doorway). An in-house brew-master tightly edits the all-natural, preservative-free beers on tap. Good bar food makes the most of fresh produce from St Lawrence Market (p60) next door. (📞416-867-9499; www.cestwhat.com; 67 Front St E; ⏱11:30am-1am Sun & Mon, to 2am Tue-Sat; 🚋503, 504)

Triple A Bar BAR

12 🅐 MAP P64, B2

Join the after-work crowd for cold-beer-and-shot combos at this busy dive bar. Snag a pleather booth if you can and prepare to lose your voice (the later it is, the louder it gets). If hunger strikes, try the Texas barbecue. (📞416-850-2726; www.tripleabar.ca; 138 Adelaide St E; ⏱noon-2am; 🚌141, 143, 144, 145)

Entertainment

Reservoir Lounge JAZZ

13 ⭐ MAP P64, A3

Swing dancers, jazz singers and blues crooners call this cool, candlelit basement lounge home, and it's hosted its fair share of musical greats over the years. Where else can you enjoy a martini while dipping strawberries into chocolate fondue during the show? Tables are reserved for diners; prepare to drop at least $15 per person to sit down. (📞416-955-0887; www.reservoirlounge.com; 52 Wellington St E; cover $5-10; ⏱7:30pm-2am Tue-Sat; 🚌503, 504)

Soulpepper THEATER

14 ⭐ MAP P64, F4

This theater company has a repertoire ranging from new works to classics, with most pieces focused on the diversity of Canada's voices and identities. Youth-outreach initiatives and theater training programs are shining stars. It's housed in the **Young Centre for the Performing Arts** (📞416-866-8666; www.youngcentre.ca;

50 Tank House Lane; 📶72, 🚋503, 504) in the heart of the Distillery District. (📞416-866-8666; www.soulpepper.ca; 50 Tank House Lane; 🚋503, 504)

CanStage   THEATER

15 ⭐ MAP P64, D3

Contemporary CanStage produces top-rated Canadian and international plays by the likes of David Mamet and Tony Kushner from its own Berkeley Street Theatre. It's also behind the wonderfully accessible (pay-what-you-can) midsummer productions of Shakespeare in High Park (p119); bring a blanket, show up early and enjoy theater under the stars. (Canadian Stage Company; 📞416-368-3110; www.canstage.com; 26 Berkeley St; ⏰box office 10am-6pm Mon-Sat, show days to 8pm; 🚋503, 504)

Young People's Theatre   THEATER

16 ⭐ MAP P64, C3

Catch a show at this innovative theater that has been delivering enlightening children's plays and drama camps for more than 50 years. Despite the common misconception, the vast majority of performances are made by professional *adult* actors, not child actors. (Lorraine Kimsa Theatre for Young People; 📞416-862-2222; www.youngpeoplestheatre.ca; 165 Front St E; ⏰box office 9am-5pm; ♿; 🚋503, 504)

Shopping

Hoi Bo   DESIGN

17 🅑 MAP P64, F4

The refined clothing and accessories sold here are all handmade

---

Winter Festivals

Toronto Christmas Market (www.torontochristmasmarket.com; 9 Trinity St; Fri-Sun $6, Tue-Thu free; ⏰Tue-Sun mid-Nov–late Dec; ♿; 📶72, 🚋503, 504) The Distillery District is at its festive best from mid-November to Christmas Eve during its European-style Christmas Market, showcasing hundreds of local handcrafted products, a carousel and photo ops with Santa.

Toronto Light Festival (https://torontolightfest.com; 9 Trinity St; free; ⏰mid-Jan–early Mar; 📶72, 🚋503, 504) What better way to get over the winter blues than with a light festival featuring exhibits and performances by local and international artists? The Toronto Light Festival transforms the Distillery District into a bright urban oasis every year, making winter fun (even if it feels like -20°C outside).

Christmas Market, Distillery District (p65)

by an in-house crew using natural materials such as organic wool, bamboo and Ontario beeswax. Items aren't cheap, but they're unique and high quality. Think of them as investment pieces. Located in the Distillery District (p65). (☏647-852-5488; www.hoibo.com; 15 Trinity St; ◷11am-7pm Tue-Sat, to 6pm Sun & Mon; 🚌72, 🚋503, 504)

Corktown Designs   JEWELRY

18 🅐 MAP P64, F4

Jewelry is the focus here, with case upon glass case of it. Find unique work by locally based artisans and some international folks. Handbags and accessories sold, too. (☏416-861-3020; www.corktowndesigns.com; 5 Trinity St; ◷10am-7pm Mon-Wed, to 8pm Thu, to 9pm Fri & Sat, 11am-6pm Sun; 🚌72, 🚋503, 504)

Top Experience 📷
Go birdwatching in Tommy Thompson Park

Once a thin spit of land, Tommy Thompson Park was created when more than 6,500,000 cu meters of sand and silt from the development of Toronto's outer harbor was relocated here. It's a haven for birds – over 316 species have been spotted – and the park is a great place for an outdoorsy walk. Bring binoculars if you can!

☎ 416-661-6600

www.tommythompson
park.ca

Leslie St

🕐 4-9pm Mon-Fri,
5:30am-9pm Sat & Sun

🚌 83 Jones S, 🚋 501

Nature Trails

Though Tommy Thompson Park has 18km of trails, only 3.3km are nature trails. Narrow and ungraded, they cross through meadows and along wetlands, affording many more opportunities to see birds and other wildlife than the paved or graded-gravel trails. From the parking lot, follow the multi-use trail until you reach the marina, where the park's first, and longest, nature trail splits off.

Guided Walks

On weekends enthusiastic staff members lead two guided tours through Tommy Thompson Park. The Wildlife Walk typically crosses forests, meadows and wetlands and includes an overview of the park's history and its flora and fauna; the Bird Walk focuses on the park's remarkable birdlife, taking participants to prime bird-watching spots (BYO binoculars). Walks take approximately two hours and leave at 10am from the Nature Centre. Be sure to register online. There's no set fee, but donations are encouraged.

Lighthouse Views

Although the lighthouse itself isn't particularly noteworthy, its position at the tip of Tommy Thompson Park means it has breathtaking views of the Toronto Islands and Toronto's skyline beyond. Located at the end of a pedestrian path, it lies a 10km round-trip from the entrance – a decent walk. Be sure to take provisions!

★ Top Tips

o Birds are visible year-round but are most abundant in May and September, when migration is heaviest.

o The park's paths have relatively little shade, and there's nowhere to buy water or other supplies. Bring a brimmed hat and plenty of water.

o Many locals refer to the park by its old name: the Leslie St Spit, or just 'the Spit.'

✕ Take a Break

Stop at **Gale's Snack Bar** (539 Eastern Ave; meals $2-4; ⏰10am-6pm Mon-Fri, to 5pm Sat; 🚋501, 502, 503) for a quick bite or sandwiches for a picnic in the park.

Alternatively, save your taste buds for a post-visit pint and elevated pub grub at **Rorschach Brewing Co** (📞416-901-3233; www.rorschachbrewing. com; 1001 Eastern Ave; ⏰5-11pm Mon-Wed, noon-11pm Thu, to midnight Fri & Sat, to 9pm Sun; 🚋301, 501) near the park entrance.

Explore ◎

Downtown Yonge

Toronto's version of Times Sq and San Francisco's Castro district, Downtown Yonge consists of a dense urban strip. At its northern end is Toronto's main gay neighborhood – the Village – unmistakable with its rainbow crosswalks and Pride flags, and home to beloved institutions like Glad Day bookstore and Buddies in Bad Times Theatre. Toronto's distinctive City Hall, the historic Elgin & Winter Garden Theatre and the Eaton Centre mall are also here. At the southern end, the huge Yonge & Dundas Sq lights up the streets with its jumbotrons and occasionally hosts festivals.

The Short List

o **Elgin & Winter Garden Theatre (p76)** *Touring Toronto's century-old double-decker theater, the last of its kind.*

o **City Hall (p82)** *Snapping a pic in front of the iconic 'Toronto' sign with the flying saucer-like city hall in the background.*

o **Dirty Bingo at O'Grady's (p86)** *Vying for bingo glory at this friendly pub where drag queens call out the numbers.*

o **Glad Day (p88)** *Browsing the shelves at this iconic bookstore and staying on for the Saturday Night Dance Party.*

Getting There & Around

S The Yellow line has several stops along Yonge St in downtown, including Queen, Dundas, College and Wellesley stations.

Neighborhood Map on p80

Nathan Phillips Square forms the forecourt to City Hall (p82), by architect Viljo Revell MIKECPHOTO/SHUTTERSTOCK ©

Top Experience 📷

Catch a show at Elgin & Winter Garden Theatre

The world's last double-decker theater – one theater sits seven stories above the other – that's still in operation, the Elgin & Winter Garden is a sumptuously restored 1913 vaudeville theater with hand-painted walls, botanical-themed ceilings, rich fabrics and gold-leaf decor. Seeing a show here, or even just touring the theater, is a classic Toronto experience.

◉ MAP P80, D8

📞 416-314-2871

www.heritagetrust.on.ca/ ewg

189 Yonge St; **S** Queen

tours adult/student $12/10

Double-Decker Engineering

Designed by New York architect Thomas Lamb in 1913, this double-decker building is an engineering feat: the domed ceiling of the lower Elgin Theatre is suspended by steel rods from the floor of the upper Winter Garden Theatre, high above. As you crane your neck to admire the Elgin's gilded dome, imagine all that lies on the other side!

Winter Garden Floral Ceiling

The Winter Garden Theatre's ceiling is a unique and magical part of the venue's country-garden theme. Based on the original decor, it's made up of more than 5000 beech branches and leaves that were harvested, preserved and painted before being woven into a wire grid high above the seats.

Winter Garden Murals

Two thousand sq meters of original watercolor murals of garden roses, morning glories, ivy and trellises cover the walls of the Winter Garden Theatre – they're impossible to miss. During the theater's restoration in the late 1980s, workers used hundreds of kilograms of bread dough to clean the delicate works of art.

Vaudeville Sets

The Elgin & Winter Garden's array of vaudeville-scenery sets is the largest collection of its kind in the world. Dating from 1913 to 1918, the sets were stowed away in the Winter Garden when it closed in 1928. Custom-made and hand painted at Loew's Scenic Studios in NYC, the sets were discovered during the theater's renovation in the 1980s – a once-in-a-lifetime find. Each theater had its own collection with interchangeable cloth flats, many integrating the art deco and art nouveau styles popular during the vaudeville era. Several are on display in the Theatre Centre.

★ Top Tips

o Avoid the $10-per-ticket service charge by purchasing tickets directly at the box office.

o Rush tickets are available for select shows starting at 9am on performance days; there's a maximum of two tickets per order.

o Tours are cash only; no need to reserve in advance.

✕ Take a Break

Senator Restaurant (p84) has stylish art deco decor and serves home-style classics such as meat loaf, and fish-and-chips.

For something quick, the Eaton Centre's Urban Eatery (p84) is across the street from the theaters, and has more than 45 eateries.

Theatre History

The Elgin & Winter Garden Theatres, elegant and plush, were built to serve as the Canadian flagship of the Loew's chain of vaudeville theaters. Each was designed with a different audience in mind: the Winter Garden Theatre, the upper and more exclusive one, had big-ticket shows and reserved seating. The Elgin Theatre (then called Loew's Yonge Street Theatre) was much larger, with more than 1500 seats, and was used for less-renowned acts and silent films. Despite the theaters' initial popularity, the advent of talkies (pictures with sound) led to the closure of the Winter Garden just 15 years after it opened. It remained shuttered for over 50 years. Meanwhile, the Elgin was converted into a movie house, and by the 1970s it was used mostly to screen low-budget films.

Enter the Ontario Heritage Trust. Tasked with protecting and preserving Canada's cultural heritage, the government agency purchased the property in 1981. A year later the theaters were designated a national historic site. The trust spearheaded efforts to restore them, raising $29 million in private and public funds. Though the Elgin quickly re-emerged as a legitimate venue (a successful production of Broadway musical *Cats* ran from 1985 to 1987), the trust closed the theaters for complete restoration and renovation. The project lasted three years – but it was worth the wait. Today the theaters serve as reminders of the city's past through sumptuous color and delightful detail.

Left: Winter Garden Theatre

Downtown Yonge

Downtown Yonge

For reviews see

○	Top Experiences	p76
○	Sights	p82
⊗	Eating	p83
○	Drinking	p86
○	Entertainment	p88
○	Shopping	p88

Allan Gardens

Pembroke St

George St

Jarvis St

Mutual St

Gerrard St E

Dalhousie St

Dundas St E

Church St

Shuter St

Bond St

Queen St E

Richmond St E

Granby St

Church St

Gerrard St E

Gould St

Ryerson Polytechnic University

Yonge & Dundas Sq

Victoria St

⊗10

20 ○

○

21 ○

Elgin & Winter Garden Theatre

Yonge St

Queen St

Yonge St

⊗ ⊗4

7 ⊗

Yonge St

Dundas St

Edward St

⊗8

○3

25 ○

Bay St

Barbara Ann Scott Park

LaPlante Ave

Toronto General Hospital

Gerrard St W

Bay St

Toronto Coach Terminal

Elizabeth St

Church of the Holy Trinity

Trinity Sq

James St

Albert St

Bay St

Hagerman St

○1 City Hall

Nathan Phillips Sq

Queen St W

York St

Osgoode

Dundas St W

Shephard St

Chestnut St

Elm St

Centre Ave

○2

Armoury St

Textile Museum of Canada

University Ave

St Patrick

Simcoe St

Simcoe St

St Patrick St

Orde St

Murray St

McCaul St

Henry St

McCaul St

BALDWIN VILLAGE

Baldwin St

D'Arcy St

Pow Wow Café (800m) →

Art Gallery of Ontario

Grange Park

○7

Stephanie St

John St

ENTERTAINMENT DISTRICT

Renfrew Pl

Pullan Pl

Richmond St W

A B C D E F

5 6 7 8

Sights

City Hall
HISTORIC BUILDING

1 ⊙ MAP P80, C7

Much-maligned City Hall was Toronto's bold leap into architectural modernity. Its twin clamshell towers, central 'flying saucer', ramps and mosaics were completed in 1965 to Finnish architect Viljo Revell's award-winning design. Frank Lloyd Wright compared it to a gravestone; Revell died before construction was finished. Collect a self-guided tour pamphlet from the info desk; don't miss the stunning artwork by Norval Morrisseau, one of Canada's most revered indigenous painters. (📞311, 416-392-2489; www.toronto.ca; 100 Queen St W; free; ⏱8:30am-4:30pm Mon-Fri; 🅿; 🚇Queen)

Church of the Holy Trinity

Textile Museum of Canada
MUSEUM

2 ⊙ MAP P80, B7

Tucked into a condo tower, this small museum has exhibits drawing on its permanent collection of more than 13,000 items from Latin America, Africa, Europe, Southeast Asia and India, as well as contemporary Canada. Workshops teach batik making, weaving, knitting and needlecraft; many are included in the price of admission. (📞416-599-5321; www.textilemuseum.ca; 55 Centre Ave; adult/child $15/free, 5-8pm Wed by donation; ⏱11am-5pm Thu-Tue, to 8pm Wed, tours 2pm Sun; 🚇St Patrick)

Church of the Holy Trinity
CHURCH

3 ⊙ MAP P80, D7

Tucked away behind the west side of the gargantuan Eaton Centre (p89) is the oasis-like Trinity Sq, named after the welcoming Anglican Church of the Holy Trinity. When it opened in 1847 it was the first church in Toronto not to charge parishioners for pews. Today, it's notable for welcoming same-sex marriage ceremonies and is a cross between a house of worship, a small concert venue and a community drop-in center – everything a downtown church should be! (📞416-598-4521; www.holytrinitytoronto.org; 10 Trinity Sq; ⏱11am-3pm Mon-Fri, 8am-2pm Sun; services 12:15pm Wed, 10:30am & 2pm Sun; 🚇Dundas)

COREY WISE/LONELY PLANET ©

Local Experiences

Drag queens

Dirty Bingo at **O'Grady's** (p86) and Sunday Drag Brunch at **Glad Day** (p88) are the most popular of the many drag-related events in the Village. (Arrive early!)

Outdoor eats

In the warmer months, join office workers and students for lunch at Fresh Wednesdays in front of **City Hall** or the **Outdoor Eateries** (p82) near Ryerson University.

Shopping

Instead of hitting the international chains in the **Eaton Centre** (p89), do as locals do and hit the neighborhood shops, like **Dead Dog Records** (p89).

Eating

Outdoor Eateries   FOOD TRUCK $

4 ⊗ MAP P80, D6

Food trucks, repurposed shipping containers and plywood sheds make up this outdoor food court at the heart of Yonge St. Short-order cooks prep burritos, Philly cheese-steak subs, crepes, vegan eats and more. Hungry diners (many of them students from nearby Ryerson University) fill the picnic tables in the center courtyard. Twinkling lights set the mood in the evening. (335 Yonge St; mains from $3; ⏰11am-10:30pm; ⊘; Ⓢ Dundas, College)

Loblaw's   SUPERMARKET $

5 ⊗ MAP P80, E4

Yeah, it's a grocery-store chain, but this flagship is a must-stop for its high-quality prepared-foods section: sushi made to order, grilled meats, thin-crust pizza, creative sandwiches and salads... and don't miss the killer patisserie and Wall of Cheese. Plenty of seating and occasional live music. Ninety minutes of free parking, too. (☎416-593-6154; 60 Carlton St; mains from $3; ⏰7am-11pm; Ⓟ ⊘; Ⓢ College)

Okonomi House   JAPANESE $

6 ⊗ MAP P80, C1

Okonomi House is one of the only places in Toronto, and perhaps North America, dishing up authentic *okonomiyaki* (savory Japanese cabbage pancakes filled with meat, seafood or vegetables). It's not fancy – just a step up from a diner – but it's a must for Japanophiles. (☎416-925-6176; 23 Charles St W; mains $9-17; ⏰11:30am-3pm & 4:30-10pm Mon-Fri, noon-3pm & 4:30-10pm Sat; ⊘; Ⓢ Bloor-Yonge)

Doors Open Toronto

Over the fourth weekend of May, several public and private buildings of architectural and historical significance creak open their doors, allowing you to sneak a free peek at what's hot and what's not in other people's digs. Book ahead for walking tours and big-name buildings such as **City Hall** (p82) and **Union Station** (p47).

Salad King   THAI $

7 MAP P80, D6

An institution among students of neighboring Ryerson University, the colorful and somewhat misleadingly named Salad King dispenses large bowls of standard Thai curries, noodle soups, rice and, yes, salads, for around $12. Long stainless-steel shared tables and cozy booths are usually full of hungry patrons. You can specify your desired level of spice on a scale of one to 20! (☎416-593-0333; www.saladking.com; 340 Yonge St; mains $11-13; ⏱11am-10pm Mon-Thu, to 11pm Fri, noon-11pm Sat, to 9pm Sun; ☝; ⑤Dundas)

Urban Eatery   FOOD HALL $

8 MAP P80, D7

More than just a food court, the Urban Eatery, in the basement of the gargantuan Eaton Centre (p89), has more than 45 outlets, from fast food to seated dining. If you're in a pinch for something to eat and you're tired of walking, you're bound to find something here; in fact, you'll be spoiled for choice. (1 Dundas St W; mains from $5; ⏱10am-9pm Mon-Sat, to 7pm Sun; 📶☝; ⑤Dundas)

Smith   CANADIAN $$

9 MAP P80, E2

Come to this bohemian-chic eatery in the heart of the Village for brunch, when the classics are served with flair: eggs Benedict with leek fondue, a short stack with maple cream cheese and candied lemon, or perhaps a Bloody Mary with a bouquet of bacon on top. Is your mouth watering yet? Reservations recommended. (☎416-926-2501; http://smithrestaurant.com; 553 Church St; mains $18-28; ⏱11am-4pm & 5-11pm Tue-Thu, to midnight Fri, 9am-4pm & 5pm-midnight Sat, 9am-4pm Sun; ☝; ⑤Wellesley)

Senator Restaurant   DINER $$

10 MAP P80, D7

Art deco buffs will delight in the Senator's curved glass windows, fluted aluminum counter face and original booths. Meals are refreshingly simple and home style: the fish-and-chips, meat loaf and macaroni are especially recommended. On weekends, head upstairs to its wine bar, **Top O' the Senator**, for drinks and live jazz until midnight. (☎416-364-7517; www.thesenator.com; 249 Victoria St;

mains $18-36; ⏱7:30am-2:30pm Mon. to 9pm Tue-Fri, 8am-2:30pm & 4:30-9pm Sat, 8am-2:30pm Sun; **S** Dundas)

Hair of the Dog PUB FOOD **$$**

11 MAP P80, E4

At its best in the warmer months, when two levels of shaded patio spring to life with a gay and straight crowd, this chilled puppy is delightfully less mainstream than its Village neighbors a few blocks north. Equally tempting as a drinking venue, the Dog serves great sharing plates and salads, too. No nonvegetarian can possibly resist the butter-chicken grilled cheese. (📞416-964-2708; www.hairofdogpub.com; 425 Church St; share plates $12-20, mains $15-24; ⏱11:30am-midnight Mon-Thu, to 2am Fri, 10:30am-2am Sat, to midnight Sun; **S** College)

Wish Restaurant CANADIAN **$$**

12 MAP P80, D2

There's no need to get out of the city to experience beach vibes. Wish is a South Beach–inspired restaurant serving up delicious Canadian comfort food and brunch, including lots of vegetarian and vegan options. The gorgeous patio is heated during the colder months, so you can enjoy it year-round. (📞416-935-0240; http://wishintoronto.com; 3 Charles St E; mains $19-22; ⏱11:30am-11pm Tue-Fri, 10am-3pm & 5-11pm Sat, 10am-4pm Sun; 🏖; **S** Bloor-Yonge)

Summer patio dining in downtown Toronto

First Nations
Heritage & History

Toronto is built on the ancestral lands of several First Nations communities: the Mississauga of the New Credit, the Anishnabeg, the Chippewa, the Wendat and the Haudenosaunee. The latter's name translates roughly as 'people who live in the extended longhouses'; indeed, indigenous communities in this region were known for their distinctive curved-roof houses, covered in bark and animal skins, and up to 100m long – space enough for the 20 family 'apartments' within.

Indigenous warriors were recruited into various conflicts between French, British and American colonists, often to decisive effect. But their communities were repaid in misery, including broken treaties, starvation and disease; today more than 90% of First Nations Torontonians live at or below poverty level. First Nations activists have won important victories in their long fight to expose and rectify ancient (and not-so-ancient) wrongs; prime ministers have apologized for cultural genocide, a Truth and Reconciliation Commission laid out a series of recommendations, and legal damages have been paid to survivors of forced adoptions, residential schools and other atrocities.

The exact population of First Nations people in Toronto is difficult to determine; the latest census says 45,000, but service agencies say it's closer to 70,000. Of course, the cultures of First Nations peoples are more than their wrenching history; they're also art, food, celebrations and more, with many First Nations' locales dotting the city. Check out **Pow Wow Café** (p97) for traditional food, the **Art Gallery of Ontario** (p92) for works of art, and **Native Canadian Centre of Toronto** (p109) for weekly cultural events and seasonal powwows.

Drinking

O'Grady's
PUB

13 🚇 MAP P80, E3

Come to this friendly Irish pub on Wednesdays for Dirty Bingo nights, when fabulous drag queens call out numbers and give winners risqué prizes from 9pm to midnight. On bingo-less nights, it's all about the patio – the Village's largest – which fills up as soon as the sun comes out. The kitchen, serving comfort food, stays open late. (📞 416-323-2822; www.ogradyschurch.com; 517 Church St; ⏱ 11am-2am; **S** Wellesley)

One Eighty

BAR

14 MAP P80, C1

Swanky and priced to match, the city's highest licensed patio has arguably Toronto's best views outside the CN Tower. It's in the Manulife Centre, a mall and residential building, and unlike the tower, it has no admission fee, though you're well advised to drop some cash on a martini or a meal. Look for the elevators next to the Cineplex. (416-967-0000; www.the51stfloor.com; Manulife Centre, 55 Bloor St W, 51st fl; 5pm-midnight Mon-Thu, to 2am Fri & Sat, 11am-midnight Fri-Sun; S Bay)

Storm Crow Manor

BAR

15 MAP P80, E2

Geek out at this Victorian mansion turned bar with sci-fi themed rooms, board games and dungeon masters. Drinks come in all shapes and sizes, including beakers and Darth Vadar heads (dry ice and light-up ice cubes figure strongly). Hearty pub grub is served; roll the dice, literally, to pick your meal and sides. (416-367-2769; www.stormcrow.com; 580 Church St; 11am-11pm Sun-Wed, to midnight Thu, to 2am Fri & Sat; S Wellesley)

Crews & Tangos

BAR

16 MAP P80, E4

A sprawling bar that becomes a crowded nightclub on weekends, Crews & Tangos features live drag and cabaret shows and DJs out back. Boys who like boys, girls who like girls, girlish boys and boyish girls and all their friends tend to make up the lively crowd in this welcoming space. Look for the blue brick house with the murals. (647-349-7469; www.crewsandtangos.com; 508 Church St; 8pm-2am Sun-Fri, 6pm-2am Sat; S Wellesley)

Black Eagle

GAY

17 MAP P80, E4

Men-only Eagle lures leather-men, uniform fetishists and their admirers. The year-round rooftop patio is the perfect place to meet a Daddy: Sunday-afternoon barbecues draw a strong crowd. There's a cruising area upstairs and a renovated dance area downstairs. While it's not for the fainthearted, the folks here are generally as friendly as they come. (416-413-1219; www.blackeagletoronto.com; 457 Church St; 3pm-3am Mon-Sat, to midnight Sun; S Wellesley)

LGBTIQ+ Pride Fest

Pride Toronto (www.pridetoronto.com; Jun) is one of the city's most well-attended festivals, celebrating diversity of sexuality and gender identity with a whole month of community events, workshops and gatherings – all mostly free. The celebration ends big with a Trans March, Dyke March and Pride Parade, when the streets around the Village heave with over a million revelers.

Woody's/Sailor
BAR

18 🚇 MAP P80, E4

Toronto's most well-known gay bar is a sprawling complex with a grab bag of tricks, from drag shows, 'best ass' contests and billiard tables to nightly DJs. Sailor is a slick bar off to one side. Popular with the 30- and 40-something crowd. (📞416-972-0887; www.woodystoronto.com; 465-467 Church St; 🕐1pm-2am; Ⓢ Wellesley)

Entertainment

Buddies in Bad Times Theatre
THEATER

19 ⭐ MAP P80, D4

Founded in 1979, Buddies is the world's oldest queer theater company. Its mission: to develop and produce queer voices and stories on stage. Check the website for programming: pay-what-you-can tickets are available for some shows. Late night on weekends the theater opens its bar, **Tallulah's**, where proceeds from dance parties, drag shows and other events are used to support the theater. (📞416-975-8555; http://buddiesinbadtimes.com; 12 Alexander St; Ⓢ Wellesley)

Ed Mirvish Theatre
THEATER

20 ⭐ MAP P80, D7

Formerly the Canon, the Ed Mirvish Theatre was renamed in 2011 in honor of the late Ed Mirvish, a well-loved Toronto businessman, philanthropist and patron of the arts. One of four Mirvish theaters, the 1920s-era vaudeville hall is a hot ticket for musical extravaganzas. Rush tickets are available for same-day performances only and are limited to two per person. (📞416-872-1212; www.mirvish.com; 244 Victoria St; Ⓢ Dundas)

Massey Hall
CONCERT VENUE

21 ⭐ MAP P80, D7

Few venues have hosted as diverse a range of performances as Massey Hall, with over 125 years in the business. Extensive renovations to bring the 2500-seat space into the next generation while retaining its period charm were completed in November 2021. (📞416-872-4255; www.masseyhall.com; 178 Victoria St; 🕐box office from noon show days only; Ⓢ Queen)

Shopping

Glad Day
BOOKS

22 🔒 MAP P80, E3

It's the oldest still-running gay bookstore in the world, making Glad Day an LGBTIQ+ landmark. The store has transformed from a place to defy censorship of LGBTIQ+ publications into an event and gathering space to promote creativity and further free speech. It's also a cafe and bar. Weekends mean Saturday-night dance parties and Sunday Drag Brunch. (📞416-901-6600; www.gladdaybookshop.com; 499 Church St; 🕐10am-10pm Mon-Thu, to 2am Fri & Sat, 11am-7pm Sun; Ⓢ Wellesley)

BORNAH/SHUTTERSTOCK ©

Dead Dog Records   MUSIC

23 🏠 MAP P80, E3

A small used-record store with a good, well-organized selection of vinyls, CDs and even cassette tapes. Check out the merch from long-past concerts and don't leave without digging through the $2 bins – there are finds to be had! (📞 647-325-4575; www. deaddogrecords.ca; 568 Church St; ⏰ noon-8pm Tue-Thu, 11am-7pm Sat, noon-6pm Sun; Ⓢ Wellesley)

Out on the Street   ADULT

24 🏠 MAP P80, E2

Three floors of LGBTIQ-oriented merch, sex toys and Pride Canada souvenirs. A great place to get rainbow briefs, a dildo or a Pride mug...something for everyone!

(📞 416-967-2759; 551 Church St; ⏰ 10am-8pm Mon-Wed, to 9pm Thu-Sat, 11am-7pm Sun; Ⓢ Wellesley)

Eaton Centre   MALL

25 🏠 MAP P80, D7

Located between two subway stations and opposite Yonge & Dundas Sq, downtown Toronto's largest shopping mall has branches of almost every large retailer in North America, and some not-so-well-known local stores. Constantly full of people milling about and thinning their wallets, its enormous light-filled atrium is a haven on cold winter days. (📞 416-598-8560; www.torontoeatoncentre.com; 220 Yonge St; ⏰ 10am-9:30pm Mon-Fri, 9:30am-9:30pm Sat, 10am-7pm Sun; 🛜; Ⓢ Queen, Dundas)

Kensington Market & Chinatown

Tattered around the edges, elegantly wasted Kensington Market is Toronto at its most interesting. It's not a constrained market as much as a working residential neighborhood. You'll find flavors from around the world and pocket-size vintage stores, bikers and dreadlocked urbanites, artists and anarchists getting along just fine. Adjacent to Kensington Market, straddling busy Spadina Ave, is Chinatown, with its hectic restaurants, small groceries and curio shops.

The Short List

○ **Art Gallery of Ontario (p92)** *Ogling an impressive collection of artwork from all over Canada.*

○ **Foodie heaven (p96)** *Noshing on dishes from across the world, from Hong Kong congee to Baja-style fish tacos.*

○ **Vintage shopping (p100)** *Discovering vintage clothing, accessories and more at sought-after thrift shops.*

○ **Live music (p99)** *Listening to live music at neighborhood performance spaces like the legendary Horseshoe Tavern, still drawing crowds after 70 years.*

Getting There & Around

Ⓢ The Yellow line has several stops along the eastern edge of the neighborhood.

🚋 Streetcars 310 and 510 run north–south on Spadina Ave, 505 runs east–west along Dundas St, and 306 and 506 run east–west along College St.

Neighborhood Map on p94

Cycling through Kensington Market
MARC BRUXELLE/ALAMY STOCK PHOTO ©

Top Experience 📷

Find the maker station at Art Gallery of Ontario

A work of art itself, the Art Gallery of Ontario is a spectacular building reminiscent of a crystal ship. It holds a remarkable collection of more than 80,000 works, with a focus on Canadian art from colonial times to the present. There are several floors, corridors and galleries, so consider taking a free tour to help you navigate the place.

◎ MAP P94, G4

AGO

www.ago.net

317 Dundas St W

adult/under 25yr $25/ free, 6-9pm Wed free

⊙ 10:30am-5pm Tue & Thu, to 9pm Wed & Fri, to 5:30pm Sat & Sun

🚋 505

Indigenous & Canadian Art Collection

Set on the 1st and 2nd floors, the AGO's Indigenous & Canadian Art collection is a must-see. Spanning centuries, it includes works by some of the country's greats: from landscapes by Tom Thomson and the Group of Seven to huge canvases by First Nations painter Norval Morrisseau. The range of pieces – sculptures, carvings, wall hangings, photographs, works on paper – is astounding.

Henry Moore Sculpture Centre

Opened in 1974, the 2nd-floor Henry Moore Sculpture Centre houses the world's largest public collection of this monumental artist's creations: more than 900 sculptures and works on paper. Most of the pieces were donated to the AGO by Moore himself – a remarkable gift. Allow some time to take in the artist's works and explore the multimedia exhibits that share the inspiration behind the art.

Architecture & Design

As notable as the works of art inside, the AGO building itself is well worth admiring. The original building, dating from 1900, has been renovated and expanded several times. Perhaps the most striking update was the 2008 redesign by renowned Canadian architect Frank Gehry. The almost dreamlike new elements include the stunning entrance, a curving glass wall reminiscent of a crystal ship that reflects the Victorian houses across the way; the Walker Court's spiraling **baroque staircase**, a wooden curlicue rising through a glass ceiling seemingly to the clouds; and the breathtaking **Galleria Italia**, its tall, curving wooden beams and floor-to-ceiling windows calling to mind the hull of a ship or the inside of a whale.

★ Top Tips

◦ Excellent museum tours, from hour-long overviews to 10-minute 'On the Dot' discussions about a single artwork, are always free with admission.

◦ AGO has terrific youth programming, including two roving maker stations and engaging DIY art projects in the Dr Mariano Elia Hands-On Centre.

◦ Admission is free on Wednesday evenings; arrive after 6pm and leave your backpack at the hotel to avoid queues.

◦ Admission is always free for anyone aged 25 and under.

✕ Take a Break

The museum's upscale **AGO Bistro** specializes in innovative dishes, often designed to pair with a special exhibit.

For a mid-visit cappuccino, stop at the **Espresso Bar** in **Galleria Italia**, a gorgeous, light-filled room reminiscent of the hull of a ship.

A   B   College St   C   D

For reviews see

⊙	Top Experiences	p92
✕	Eating	p96
⊖	Drinking	p98
★	Entertainment	p99
🔒	Shopping	p100

Oxford St

20

Nassau St

KENSINGTON MARKET

Baldwin St   ✕9

Leonard Ave   Bellevue Ave   Augusta Ave   Spadina Ave   Glasgow St

✕6

✕ 4   13   St Andrew St

Bellevue Square Park   ✕3

Carlyle St   Wales Ave   8   Kensington Ave

Denison Ave   ⊖11   5 ✕   ✕7

18🔒   **CHINATOWN**

Dundas St W   ✕1

Alexandra Park

Larch St

Carr St

Ryerson Ave   Denison Ave   Augusta Ave   Cameron St   Spadina Ave

🔒19

16 ★

Wolseley St

Ace La

12 ⊖   10 ⊖   Vanauley St   **QUEEN WEST**   14 ★

2 17

Queen St W

Ⓟ

A   B   C   D

Kensington Market & Chinatown

University of Toronto
(St George Campus)

College St

Queens Park

E F G H

0 — 400 m
0 — 0.2 miles

Ross St

Cecil St

Huron St

Beverley St

Henry St

Orde St

McCaul St

Murray St

University Ave

BALDWIN
VILLAGE

Baldwin St

Elm St

D'Arcy St

Dundas St W   21

Art Gallery
of Ontario

St Patrick

Grange Ave

Grange Pl

Beverley St

Grange
Park

McCaul St

St Patrick St

Simcoe St

University Ave

Sullivan St

Huron St

Phoebe St

Stephanie St

Bulwer St

Soho St

22

John St

ENTERTAINMENT
DISTRICT

Renfrew Pl

Pullan Pl

Queen St W   15   Osgoode

E F G H

Eating

House of Gourmet   HONG KONG $

1 MAP P94, D4

A popular, fluorescent-bulb-lit restaurant specializing in Hong Kong–style congee, noodles, barbecue and seafood – more than 800 dishes of them! (It takes two menus with tiny font to cover the options.) Food comes out fast and piping hot. Service is equally brisk. If in doubt, try the wonton-brisket-noodle soup, a late-night fave with chunks of tender brisket and loads of noodles. (📞416-640-0103; http:// houseofgourmet.blogspot.com; 484 Dundas St W; mains $8-19; ⏰8am-2am; 🚲; 🚇310, 510)

Parka Food Co.   VEGAN

2 MAP P94, C6

A starkly white, casual restaurant serving insanely delicious vegan comfort food: burgers made from marinated portobello mushrooms and blackened cauliflower; mac 'n' (vegan) cheese with toppings like truffle mushroom and garlic and onion; and thick, flavorful soups. Everything's made in-house, from scratch, using locally sourced ingredients. Lots of gluten-free options, too. (📞416-603-3363; www. parkafoodco.com; 424 Queen St W; ⏰11:30am-9pm Mon-Thu, to 10pm Fri, noon-10pm Sat, to 8pm Sun; 🚲)

Budget eats in Kensington Market

Pow Wow Café   NATIVE AMERICAN

3 MAP P94, B3

A cozy, boho eatery with street-front seating, Pow Wow serves Ojibwe dishes, mostly fry-bread tacos with a choice of fillings such as beef chili, veggie, coconut-curry chicken or pork souvlaki. Start with a bowl of corn soup with smoked duck or order a salad with edible flowers. Cash only. (✆416-551-7717; 213 Augusta Ave; tacos from $15; ⏱11am-8pm; 🚌310, 510)

Seven Lives   TACOS $

4 MAP P94, C3

What started as a pop-up taqueria is now a hole-in-the-wall place with lines of people snaking out the door, waiting to order Baja-style fish tacos: light and flaky mahi-mahi with pico de gallo, cabbage and a creamy sauce. Other seafood and veggie combos offered, too. Most diners eat standing or take their meal to nearby Bellevue Sq. (✆416-803-1086; 69 Kensington Ave; tacos from $6; ⏱noon-6pm Mon-Fri, to 7pm Sat & Sun; 🚌310, 510)

Nguyen Huong   SANDWICHES $

5 MAP P94, D3

Cheap and delicious filled Vietnamese sandwiches are the order of the day at the original precursor to Toronto's banh mi (baguettes filled with pâté, cilantro, pork and pickled veg) phenomenon. Takeout only. (✆416-599-4625; www.nguyen huong.ca; 322 Spadina Ave; sandwiches from $3; ⏱8:30am-8:30pm; 🚌510)

Street ARToronto

While there's definitely a singular pleasure in 'discovering' street art on unexpected buildings and down random alleys, for a more purposeful exploration check out StART's website (https://streetartoronto.ca). It includes a super-handy database and map, with the locations of hundreds of paintings and murals, searchable by neighborhood.

Mother's Dumplings   CHINESE $

6 MAP P94, D1

The cleanest and best located of Chinatown's dumpling houses prepares plump and juicy dumplings to authentic recipes passed on down generations. However you like them – steamed or panfried; pork, chicken, beef, shrimp or vegetarian – these dumplings will fill your tum and delight your wallet. Always busy. (✆416-217-2008; www.mothersdumplings.com; 421 Spadina Ave; 10 dumplings from $11; ⏱11:30am-10pm Sun-Thu, to 10:30pm Fri & Sat; 🍴; 🚌506, 510)

Swatow   CHINESE $

7 MAP P94, D3

Catering to a late-night crowd with cuisine from Swatow, a city now known as Shantou, in China's Guangdong province. The house noodles are fiery, prepared in a style nicknamed 'red cooking' for its

Local Experiences

Eating late

Late-night dining in Chinatown is definitely a thing; head to **House of Gourmet** (p96) to rub elbows with locals of all stripes.

Grazing

Kensington Market is a parade of hole-in-the-wall eateries, such as **Seven Lives** (p97) and **Dipped Donuts**. Move from place to place trying different flavors and cuisines.

Parking

During the week there are often open spots in the **parking garage** on Baldwin near Kensington. On weekends, don't bother driving. Streetcars stop along Spadina, just a block away.

potent splashes of fermented rice wine. Cash only; be ready to queue. (📞416-977-0601; 309 Spadina Ave; mains $8-16; ⏱11am-2am; 🚋505, 510)

FIKA Cafe   CAFE $

8 🍴 MAP P94, C3

Meaning 'coffee break' in Swedish, FIKA is a small cafe in a turquoise Victorian house with soothing decor: exposed-brick walls, white-washed wood and artful touches such as wallpaper made of books. The menu's limited (including fresh salads and sandwiches), but its coffee and homemade-pastries are impressive. Try the cinnamon buns. (www.fika.ca; 28 Kensington Ave; mains from $6; ⏱10am-6pm Mon-Sat; 📶🅿; 🚋310, 510)

Dipped Donuts   BAKERY $

9 🍴 MAP P94, C2

A *tiny* shop selling freshly made, light, moist and fluffy doughnuts

with innovative toppings and glazes. Not into lemon-poppyseed glaze with blueberry-mint drizzle? How about rosewater pistachio nut or chocolate ganache with cookie crumble? Apple fritters, with big chunks of apple, are sold on weekends. Vegan doughnuts sold, too. Come early...the goodies often sell out. Cash only. (📞647-906-3668; www.dippeddonuts.ca; 161 Baldwin St; doughnuts from $3.25; ⏱10am-6pm Sun-Thu, to 7pm Fri & Sat; 🚋310, 510)

Drinking

BarChef   COCKTAIL BAR

10 🍸 MAP P94, B6

You'll hear 'oohs' and 'aahs' coming from the tables in the intimate near-darkness of this swanky bar as cocktails emerge alongside a bonsai tree, or under a bell jar of vanilla and hickory-wood smoke. Beyond novelty, drinks show incredible, enticing complexity without overwhelming some unique flavors – truffle snow, chamomile syrup, cedar air, and soil! (📞416-868-4800; www.barcheftoronto.com; 472 Queen St W; cocktails $16-55; 🕐6pm-2am; Ⓢ Osgoode)

Handlebar
BAR

11 🚇 MAP P94, B3

A jolly little spot paying homage to the bicycle and its lovers, from owners with a fine pedigree. In a great spot in south Kensington Market, there's some wonderful retro styling and a nice mix of shiny happy punters. A calendar of quirky hipster events makes it an easier bar to visit if you're traveling solo. (📞647-748-7433; www.thehandlebar.ca; 159 Augusta Ave; 🕐7pm-2am; 🚌505)

Velvet Underground
CLUB

12 🚇 MAP P94, A6

The place for those who prefer not to spend their nights listening to overplayed top-40 songs. Formerly an industrial club, it's the spot to get your alt-rock on, with DJs and live bands. (📞647-351-9001; http://thevelvet.ca; 508 Queen St W; 🚌501)

Moonbean Coffee Company
COFFEE

13 🚇 MAP P94, C3

'Nothing here is just ordinary,' says the dude behind the counter, and that's true. Serving the best latte west of Yonge St, Moonbean has organic and fair-trade coffees, all-day breakfasts for around $6, and 'Bite Me' vegan cookies. Grind-your-own beans from $16 per pound. Looseleaf teas sold, too. (📞416-595-0327; www.moonbeam coffee.com; 30 St Andrew St; coffees from $3; 🕐7am-8pm; 🚌510)

Entertainment

Horseshoe Tavern
LIVE MUSIC

14 ⭐ MAP P94, D6

Well past its 70th birthday, the legendary Horseshoe still plays a crucial role in the development of local indie rock. This place oozes a history of good times and classic performances. Come for a beer and check it out. (📞416-598-4226; www.horseshoetavern.com; 370 Queen St W; 🕐noon-2:30am; 🚌501, 510)

Weekend Revelry

The last Sunday of the month from May to October, Augusta Ave and the surrounding streets are pedestrian only to make room for the crowds, food vendors, live music and general revelry in Kensington Market.

Rex

JAZZ

15 ⊛ MAP P94, G6

The Rex has risen from its pugilistic, blue-collar past to become an outstanding jazz and blues venue. Over a dozen Dixieland, experimental and other local and international acts knock over the joint each week. Cheap drinks; affordable cover. (📞416-598-2475; www.therex.ca; 194 Queen St W; 🕐shows 6:30pm & 9:30pm Mon-Thu, 4pm, 6:30pm & 9:45pm Fri, noon, 3:30pm, 7pm & 9:45pm Sat & Sun; 🚋501)

Theatre Passe Muraille

THEATER

16 ⊛ MAP P94, A6

Since the 1960s the Theatre Passe Muraille, in the old Nasmith's Bakery & Stables, has focused on radical new plays with contemporary Canadian themes. Post-performance chats with the cast and producers occur often. Saturday and Sunday matinees are pay what you can. (Theater Beyond Walls; 📞416-504-7529; www.passemuraille. on.ca; 16 Ryerson Ave; 🕐Oct-Apr; 🚋501)

Cameron House

LIVE MUSIC

17 ⊛ MAP P94, C6

Singer-songwriters, soul, jazz and country performers grace this boho stage; artists, musos, dreamers and slackers crowd both front and back rooms. Look for the building with the colorful murals. (📞416-703-0811; www.thecameron. com; 408 Queen St W; 🕐4pm-2am Mon-Sat, 6pm-2am Sun; 🚋501, 510)

Shopping

Courage My Love

VINTAGE

18 🔒 MAP P94, C4

Vintage-clothing stores have been around Kensington Market for decades, but Courage My Love amazes fashion mavens with its secondhand slip dresses, retro pants and white dress shirts in a cornucopia of styles. The beads, buttons, leather goods and silver jewelry are handpicked. Well stocked without being overwhelming. (📞416-979-1992; 14 Kensington Ave; 🕐11am-6pm Mon-Sat, 1-5pm Sun; 🚋505, 510)

Sonic Boom

MUSIC

19 🔒 MAP P94, D5

The largest indie record store in Canada, Sonic Boom has rows upon rows of new and used vinyl, CDs and even cassettes. Longtime staffers are deeply knowledgeable, offering direction and advice. Quirky T-shirts, irreverent souvenirs and coffee-table books (most with a musical bent) are sold at the front. (📞216-532-0334; https://sonicboommusic.com; 215 Spadina Ave; 🕐10am-10pm; 🚇310, 510)

Bungalow

VINTAGE

20 🔒 MAP P94, B2

A vintage store selling well-curated home goods, furniture and clothing. Items change regularly, but expect mid-century Modern tableware, teak bowls and trays, retro sunglasses and pillbox hats. New hipster clothing and accessories also sold. (📞416-598-0204; www. bungalow.to; 273 Augusta Ave; 🕐11am-6:30pm Mon-Thu, to 8pm Fri & Sat, to 6pm Sun; 🚇306, 506)

Bay of Spirits Gallery

GIFTS & SOUVENIRS

21 🔒 MAP P94, F4

The works of Norval Morrisseau – the first indigenous artist to have a solo exhibit at the **National Gallery of Canada** (www.gallery. ca) – are proudly on display in this atmospheric space, which carries aboriginal art from across the country. Look for the Pacific West Coast totem poles (from miniature to over 4m tall), Inuit carvings and Inukshuk figurines. (📞416-971-5190; www.bayofspirits.com; 334 Dundas St W; 🕐10am-5pm Tue-Sat, noon-5pm Sun; 🚇505)

Vintage clothes, Kensington Market

MEC

SPORTS & OUTDOORS

22 🔒 MAP P94, E6

MEC is your mecca if you have a fetish for outdoor and adventure equipment. Multiple brands of backpacking, camping, hiking and travel gear line the walls of this Canadian storehouse; sign up for lifetime membership ($5) on the spot to make a purchase. The helpful staff are swamped on weekends, so try midweek if you need advice. (Mountain Equipment Co-op; 📞416-340-2667; www.mec.ca; 300 Queen St W; 🕐10am-9pm Mon-Fri, 9am-8pm Sat, 10am-6pm Sun; 🚇; 🚇Osgoode)

Explore ◈
Yorkville &
the Annex

This a district of odd bedfellows, from Yorkville's four-star hotels, luxe shopping and homes of the fabulous at the eastern end to the Annex's gritty streets, world eats and downtown residential area – the city's largest, favored by students and academics – at the western end. The students are from the prestigious University of Toronto, which forms the neighborhood's southern edge with its stately Victorian and Romanesque buildings. Nearby is the city's finest natural-history museum, as well as several other worthwhile museums.

The Short List

o **Royal Ontario Museum (p104)** Getting lost in Canada's largest and most extensive museum of natural history and world culture.

o **Hot Docs (p114)** Catching a couple of docs (or a couple of dozen) at the largest documentary festival in North America.

o **Mink Mile (p113)** Feasting your eyes on the boutiques and luxury stores in this sumptuous district, Toronto's answer to NYC's Fifth Ave.

o **Bata Shoe Museum (p108)** Marveling at the thousands of shoes and related items, some more than 4000 years old.

Getting There & Around

Ⓜ The Green line has several stops along Bloor St.

🚌 The 94A runs east–west across the district on Wellesley St/Harbord St.

Neighborhood Map on p106

Royal Ontario Museum (p104)
JHVEPHOTO/SHUTTERSTOCK © ARCHITECT: DANIEL LIBESKIND

Top Experience 📷
Discover fossils and skeletons at Royal Ontario Museum

One of the largest museums in North America, the ROM dazzles with gallery upon gallery of fossils, artifacts and art, as well as hands-on exhibits and weekly events. The building itself is fascinating: an amalgam of old and new. Come here for a day or a week – you'll likely always have more to see. Docent-led tours help unpack the place.

◎ MAP P106, E3

ROM; www.rom.on.ca

adult/child $23/14, 5:30-8:30pm 3rd Mon of month free

🕑10am-5:30pm daily, to 8:30pm 3rd Mon of month

First Peoples Art & Culture Gallery

This gallery provides insight into the works of art and cultural heritage of Canada's indigenous people from precolonial times to the present. The collection includes ceremonial clothing, birch-bark canoes, fine art and more. A small theater screens documentaries and hosts live performances, adding a present-day perspective to the collection. Knowledgeable staffers are available on weekdays to answer questions.

Hands-On Galleries

Younger visitors will appreciate ROM's two interactive galleries: the **Discovery Gallery** and the **Family Gallery of Hands-on Biodiversity**. Kids can touch shark skulls and beaver pelts, dig for dinosaur bones and walk through bat caves. Imaginative play has children hiding in foxholes and dressing up as medieval folk. Facilitators share what's on offer and answer the many questions kids have.

Mosaic Ceiling

Though ROM is filled with a dizzying number of artifacts and art, its mosaic ceiling itself is dazzling. Commissioned in 1933 by the museum's first director, the ceiling is made up of over a million Venetian tiles in myriad patterns and symbols representing the breadth of ROM's collection. Look for the Mayan temple, the Egyptian falcon, the three-clawed Chinese dragon, the bison and more.

Don't Miss

o Prehistoric skeletons in the Gallery of the Age of Mammals

o Colonial art in the Gallery of Canada

o Ceremonial masks in the Gallery of Africa, The Americas, and Asia-Pacific

o The Bat Cave

★ Top Tips

o Admission is free the third Monday evening of the month – arrive after 6pm to avoid the rush.

o Audio tours to select galleries can be downloaded from the website.

o Docent-led tours are offered daily in English and French.

o Strollers are available for rent at the coat check.

o Special exhibits are often excellent but cost extra.

✕ Take a Break

Druxy's ROM Café, the museum's basement-level cafeteria, offers burgers, sandwiches, pizza, drinks and more.

If you're looking for something a little more flash, head to nearby Trattoria Nervosa (p112) for patio dining near the Mink Mile.

★ Getting There

100 Queen's Park

S Museum

Yorkville & the Annex

For reviews see
- Top Experiences   p104
- Sights   p108
- Eating   p110
- Drinking   p112
- Entertainment   p113
- Shopping   p113

Kendal Ave

Walmer Rd

3 ⊙ ▲ ▲ ⊙ 4   C

Spadina Rd

Madoson Ave

Huron St

St George St

Admiral Rd

A 1

B 1

D 1

Albany Ave

Howland Ave

Walmer Rd

Dalton Rd

Lowther Ave

Native Canadian Centre of Toronto
6 ⊙   17 ⊗

2

Bathurst ⓢ
⊗ ⊗ 18
11

16
⊗

9
⊗

7
⊗

ⓢ Spadina

St George ⓢ

Cippincott St

19 ⊗ ⊗ 10

Borden St

Brunswick Ave

Major St

Robert St

Sussex Mews

Bloor St W

⊗ 21

1 ⊙
Bata Shoe Museum

D

Lennox St

THE ANNEX

Sussex Ave

Washington Ave

Spadina Ave

Sussex Ave

Glen Morris St

3

Harbord St

13
⊗

⊗ 8

Classic Rd

4

Lippincott St

Croft St

Borden St

Major St

Robert St

Ulster St

Willcocks St

Bancroft Ave

5

Spadina Circle

Russell St

College St

Bathurst St

Bellevue Ave

Augusta Ave

Oxford St

Spadina Ave

Glasgow St

Huron St

Ross St

Beverley St

TIFF Bell Lightbox (1.4km) ↓

6

A KENSINGTON MARKET

B

C

Cecil St

D

E Tranby Ave
F
G
H
1
Boswell Ave
Bedford Rd
Elgin Ave
Hazelton Ave
Church St
Scollard St
YORKVILLE
Yorkville Ave
Collier St
Bay St
X 12
15
Yonge St
22
Prince Arthur Ave
Avenue Rd
14 X
Asquith
2
Cumberland St
Bellair St
S Bay
Ave
Bloor-
Yonge
20
S
Royal
Bloor St W
Bloor St E
Ontario
Museum
5
St Thomas St
Balmuto St
Hayden St
2 Gardiner
Varsity
ROMBus
Museum
Charles St W
3
Stadium
S Museum
St Mary St
YONGE ST
STRIP
Isabella St
Hoskin Ave
Queen's Park Cres W
Irwin Ave
Gloucester St
Queen's
St Joseph St
St Nicholas St
4
Tower Rd
Park
Queen's Park Cres E
Dundonald St
Phipps St
Wellesley
S
University of Toronto
Wellesley St W
Wellesley St E
(St George Campus)
Breadalbane St
Maitland St
Bay St
5
King's College Rd
Yonge St
Grosvenor St
Alexander
St
Grenville St
Wood St
Queens
College S
Park
S
College St
Carlton St
6
McCaul St
University Ave
Elizabeth St
LaPlante Ave
Heritage Toronto
(1.7km)
Orde St
Toronto
General
Hospital
Barbara Ann
Scott Park
E
F
G
H

500 m
0.25 miles

Sights

Bata Shoe Museum   MUSEUM

1 ◎ MAP P106, D2

It's important in life to be well shod, a stance the Bata Shoe Museum takes seriously. Impressively designed by Raymond Moriyama to resemble a stylized shoebox, the museum houses a collection of 13,000 'pedi-artifacts' from around the globe, spanning 4500 years; only 3% to 4% are on view at any given time. Peruse 19th-century French chestnut-crushing clogs, Canadian aboriginal polar boots or famous modern pairs worn by Elton John, Indira Gandhi and Pablo Picasso. Come along for something truly different. (☎416-979-7799; www.batashoemuseum.ca; 327 Bloor St W; adult/child $14/5, 5-8pm Thu suggested donation $5; ◷10am-5pm Mon-Wed, Fri & Sat, to 8pm Thu, noon-5pm Sun; ⓢSt George)

Gardiner Museum   MUSEUM

2 ◎ MAP P106, F3

Opposite the Royal Ontario Museum (p104), the Gardiner was founded by philanthropists to house their ceramics. Spread over three floors, the collections cover several millennia; various rooms focus on 17th- and 18th-century English tavern ware, Italian Renaissance majolica, ancient American earthenware and blue-and-white Chinese porcelain. Check the website for special exhibits. Free guided tours daily at 2pm.

(☎416-586-8080; www.gardiner museum.on.ca; 111 Queen's Park; adult/child $15/free, 4-9pm Wed half-price; ◷10am-6pm Mon, Tue, Thu & Fri, to 9pm Wed, to 5pm Sat & Sun; ⓢMuseum)

Casa Loma   HISTORIC BUILDING

3 ◎ MAP P106, C1

Toronto's only castle may never have housed royalty, but it certainly has grandeur, lording over the Annex from a cliff that was once the shoreline of the glacial Lake Iroquois, from which Lake Ontario derived. A self-guided audio tour leads visitors through the four levels of the Edwardian mansion as well as the 800ft tunnel to the stables; the top floor houses a military museum. Head to the pool turned theater first, where a short film provides a good overview. (☎416-923-1171; www.casaloma. org; 1 Austin Tce; adult/child $33/23; ◷9:30am-5pm, last entry 4pm; ℗; ⓠ127, ⓢDupont)

Toronto's Artifacts

The oldest human artifact found in Toronto is a 10,000-year-old arrowhead, or Holcombe point, found in the present-day Forest Hill neighborhood. See it and many of the city's other archaeological discoveries at the **Royal Ontario Museum** (p104).

Bata Shoe Museum

Spadina Museum

MUSEUM

4 ◉ MAP P106, C1

Atop the Baldwin Steps, this gracious home and its Victorian-Edwardian gardens were built in 1866 as a country estate for financier James Austin and his family. Donated to the city in 1978, it became a museum in 1984 and was painstakingly transformed to evoke the heady age of the 1920s and '30s. Knowledgeable guides lead visitors through the estate, sharing the history of the home and the Austin family along the way – highly recommended. (☏416-392-6910; www.toronto.ca/museums; 285 Spadina Rd; tours adult/child $10/6, grounds free; ◷noon-5pm Tue-Sun Apr-Aug, noon-4pm Mon-Fri, to 5pm Sat & Sun Sep-Dec; P; Ⓢ Dupont)

ROMBus

BUS

5 ◉ MAP P106, F3

Toronto's Royal Ontario Museum (p104) organizes occasional special tours, with educated and enthusiastic guides, around historical, cultural and architectural themes. Full-day tours are either in town or within a couple of hours of it. Although they're pricey, the tours are well worth it if they pique your interest. (☏416-586-8000; www.rom.on.ca/en/whats-on/rombus; 100 Queen's Park; full-day tours $135-145; Ⓢ Museum)

Native Canadian Centre of Toronto

CULTURAL

6 ◉ MAP P106, C2

This community center hosts Thursday-night drum socials,

seasonal powwows and elders' cultural events that promote harmony and conversation between tribal members and non-indigenous people. You can also sign up for workshops and craft classes, such as beading and dancing. A **gift shop** sells hand-crafted items, including jewelry, moccasins and T-shirts. (NCCT; ☎ 416-964-9087; www.ncct.on.ca; 16 Spadina Rd; ⏱ 9am-8pm Mon-Wed, to 9pm Thu, to 6pm Fri, 10am-4pm Sat; Ⓢ Spadina)

Eating

Annex Food Hall   FOOD HALL $

7 ⊗ MAP P106, B2

Find some of the best tasty, quick eats at this industrial-chic food hall: vegan bowls, steamed-bun sandwiches, fried chicken, Bangkok-style street food, tacos and more. Order at individual counters and grab a seat at a communal picnic table. Popular with the budget-minded, especially University of Toronto students. (www.theannexfoodhall.com; 384 Bloor St W; mains $6-14; ⏱ 11:30am-9pm Sun-Wed, to 10pm Thu-Sat; Ⓢ Spadina)

Harbord Bakery   BAKERY $

8 ⊗ MAP P106, B4

A Toronto institution, this Jewish bakery has been serving customers since 1945. Stocked with all sorts of pies, cakes, cookies and bread, the challah and butter

Walking Tours 🥾

Heritage Toronto (☎ 416-338-3886; www.heritagetoronto.org; 157 King St E; suggested donation $10; ⏱ May-Oct) offers fascinating historical, cultural and nature walks, as well as bus (TTC) tours, led by museum experts, neighborhood historical-society members and emerging historians. Tours generally last one to three hours. Check the website for a handful of downloadable self-guided tours, too.

tarts are considered among the best in town. If you're hankering for a meal, check out the small prepared-foods section, with salads, sandwiches, mains...even matzo-ball soup! (☎ 416-922-5767; www.harbordbakery.ca; 115 Harbord St; from $2.75; ⏱ 8am-7pm Mon-Thu, to 6pm Fri & Sat, to 4pm Sun; 🚌 310, 510)

Fuwa Fuwa   JAPANESE $

9 ⊗ MAP P106, B2

Meaning 'Fluffy, Fluffy,' Fuwa Fuwa specializes in Japanese soufflé pancakes. Traditionally served after weddings as a sign of good fortune, here they're served daily in a small, bright-yellow eatery. The pancakes themselves are light and airy and come topped with sweet treats like tiramisu cream and coffee syrup or crème brûlée sauce and vanilla ice cream. A good dessert-for-dinner option. (☏647-618-2868; www.fuwafuwa pancakes.com; 408 Bloor St W; mains $11-16; ⊗11am-10pm Mon-Thu, to 11pm Fri, 10am-11pm Sat, to 10pm Sun; ⚲🐾; ⑤Bathurst)

Sushi on Bloor

SUSHI $

10 ✖ MAP P106, A2

Among the countless sushi restaurants on Bloor, this one stands out, its wooden booths and long tables always packed with customers enjoying platters of high-quality sushi at decent prices. Bento boxes are available, too. Great daily specials, starting at just $5, often include miso soup and salad. (☏416-516-3456; www.sushionbloor.com; 525 Bloor St W; rolls from $5.50, meals from $12; ⊗11:30am-11:30pm Mon-Thu, to midnight Fri, noon-midnight Sat, to 10pm Sun; ⑤Bathurst)

Mr Tonkatsu

JAPANESE $

11 ✖ MAP P106, A2

Asking you to grind up your own sesame-seed rice topping might just be a trick to show you how authentic this place is, but it works. The crumbed pork (or chicken) is properly crispy outside and juicy inside, and Mr Tonkatsu has that nice-but-casual vibe you find in restaurants all over Japan. (☏416-537-9000; www.mrtonkatsu.com; 530 Bloor St W; mains $12-16; ⊗11:30am-2:30pm & 4:30-10pm Mon-Sat, to 9pm Sun; ⑤Bathurst)

Yorkville & the Annex Eating

Harbord Bakery

Trattoria Nervosa   ITALIAN $$

12 🍴 MAP P106, G2

In the heart of fancy Yorkville, this restaurant is an attitude-free oasis. The patio is a good corner from which to people watch well-heeled passersby while you dig into simple, excellent pasta – the *mafalde ai funghi* has incredibly deep mushroom flavors without being overly creamy. (📞 416-961-4642; www.eatnervosa.com; 75 Yorkville Ave; mains $17-33; ⏰ 11:30am-10pm Mon-Wed, to 11pm Thu-Sat, noon-10pm Sun; 🛜 ; Ⓢ Bay)

Piano Piano   ITALIAN $$

13 🍴 MAP P106, C4

Meaning 'slowly, slowly' in Italian, Piano Piano is all about slowing down to enjoy a meal and connect with friends and family. The menu itself is traditional Italian – smoked burrata, freshly made ravioli, bone-in veal Parmesan, roasted-mushroom pizza – with plenty of vegan and gluten-free options. If you're coming with a group, ask about the 'family-style' menu. (📞 416-929-7788; www.pianopiano therestaurant.com; 88 Harbord St; mains $18-29; ⏰ noon-3pm & 5-10pm Sun-Wed, to 11pm Thu-Sat; 🍴🚻 ; 🚋 310, 510)

Sassafraz   FUSION $$$

14 🍴 MAP P106, G2

Popular with visiting celebrities and a moneyed clientele, Sassafraz epitomizes Yorkville with its elegant yet breezy decor.

Jazz combos serenade weekend brunchers, and sassy receptionists distribute diners between the sun-drenched patio and the leafy indoor courtyard. The food? Predictably good. Dress to impress. (📞 416-964-2222; www.sassafraz.ca; 100 Cumberland St; mains $22-29; ⏰ 11:30am-11pm Mon-Thu, to 1am Fri, 11am-1pm Sat, to 11pm Sun; Ⓢ Bay)

Drinking

Oxley   PUB

15 🍺 MAP P106, F2

A first-class British pub, the Oxley is located in a 19th-century row house in the heart of Yorkville. Two floors of leather seating, ornate wallpaper and Victorian-era decor fill with business folk and the well-heeled hankering for a 20oz pour of craft beer, a glass of wine or a stiff drink. Classic English fare served, too. (📞 647-348-1300; https://theoxley.com; 121 Yorkville Ave; ⏰ 11:30am-midnight Mon-Wed, to 1am Thu, to 2am Fri, 10am-2am Sat, to midnight Sun; 🛜 ; Ⓢ Bay)

Slanted Door   COFFEE

16 ☕ MAP P106, A2

A bright, contemporary coffee shop, the Slanted Door doubles as a gallery, showcasing work by emerging artists on its walls upstairs and down. The coffee drinks and teas are strong and flavorful, and the smoothies creative, with combos like apple-ginger-beet. Light snacks available, too. This is a popular place to catch up with friends or emails. (📞647-358-9888; https://slanteddor.ca; 442 Bloor St W; 🕐8:30am-7:30pm Mon-Fri, 9am-6:30pm Sat, 10am-5:30pm; 📶; Ⓢ Bathurst)

Madison Avenue Pub   PUB

17 ⭐ MAP P106, C2

Comprising three Victorian houses in the Annex, the rowdy 'Maddy' draws a late-20s University of Toronto crowd. There are billiards, darts, a sports bar, polished brass, antique-y lamps lighting the curtained upper floors, *five* patios and lots of hormones colliding. (📞416-927-1722; www.madisonavenuepub. com; 14-18 Madison Ave; 🕐11am-2am Mon-Sat, to midnight Sun; Ⓢ Spadina)

Entertainment

Hot Docs Ted
Rogers Cinema   CINEMA

18 ⭐ MAP P106, A2

This art deco theater with a two-tiered balcony screens a wonderfully varied schedule of new releases, art-house flicks, shorts,

documentaries and vintage films, and is home to the mind-expanding Hot Docs (p114) international documentary festival. (Bloor Hot Docs Cinema; 📞416-637-3123; http:// hotdocscinema.ca; 506 Bloor St W; Ⓢ Bathurst)

Lee's Palace   LIVE MUSIC

19 ⭐ MAP P106, A2

Legendary Lee's Palace has set the stage over the years for Dinosaur Jr, the Smashing Pumpkins and Queens of the Stone Age. Kurt Cobain started an infamous bottle-throwing incident when Nirvana played here in 1990. You can't miss it – look for the primary-colored mural that seems to scream out front. (📞416-532-1598; www.lees palace.com; 529 Bloor St W; 🕐8pm-2:30am; Ⓢ Bathurst)

Shopping

Mink Mile   FASHION & ACCESSORIES

20 🔒 MAP P106, G2

Often compared to NYC's Fifth Ave, Toronto's Mink Mile is home to well-known luxury stores such as Tiffany & Co, Prada, Hermès, Louis

Yorkville & the Annex Entertainment

Local Experiences

Drinking

In Yorkville, the **Oxley** is the go-to spot for after-work drinks.

Eating

Though sushi restaurants are a dime a dozen in The Annex, U of T students keep **Sushi on Bloor** (p111) packed most nights.

Hollywood North

'Hollywood North' is a name claimed by both Toronto and Vancouver. Historically, Vancouver has rights to the title – it began hosting film productions in 1910, emerging in the 1970s as a desirable alternative to LA for shooting films and TV programs, complete with tax breaks and cheaper labor. Toronto jumped into the game in the 1970s too, but it was not until the 2000s that it really came into its own. Toronto aggressively courted big-budget productions, offering generous tax incentives (some say too generous) for using local services.

It proved a great place to shoot film and TV. It has a deep and diverse pool of local acting talent; innumerable set locations, from modern cityscapes to historic buildings; and world-class production facilities, like Pinewood Toronto, which has more than 23,000 sq meters of production space and North America's largest custom sound studio. Financially, Toronto recorded over $1.25 billion in production activity in 2011, surpassing Vancouver for the first time; by 2021 the figure was $2.5 billion.

Of course, for visitors, watching films are the priority. For that, Toronto has no shortage of options. Beyond regular cinemas, Toronto hosts dozens of film-related events, most notably the **Toronto International Film Festival** (TIFF; 888-599-8433; www.tiff.net; 504), held yearly in September. It's headquartered at the **TIFF Bell Lightbox** (p55) with screenings – more than 300 in all – held at venues throughout the city. There's also **Hot Docs** (Canadian International Documentary Festival; 416-637-3123; www.hotdocs.ca; 506 Bloor St W; from $17.50; late Apr–early May; Bathurst), North America's largest documentary film festival, with more than 200 screenings held in April and May, mostly at the beautifully restored **Hot Docs Ted Rogers Cinema** (p113). And there are also many smaller niche festivals, such as LGBTIQ+ film festival **Inside Out** (Toronto LGBT Film Festival; 416-977-6847; www.insideout.ca; 350 King St W; tickets from $48; late May–early Jun; 504), and imagiNATIVE, which showcases international and Canadian indigenous filmmakers and artists.

Curious about the films made in Toronto? Big hits include:

- *The Shape of Water* (2017)
- *Spotlight* (2015)
- *Mean Girls* (2004)
- *My Big Fat Greek Wedding* (2002)
- *Good Will Hunting* (1997)

Vuitton and more. Nowhere near a mile long – it's only about 600m – it's distinguishable by its granite sidewalks, public art and mature trees. Come here to walk among the uber-wealthy or pick up some designer duds. (Bloor St W, btwn Yonge St & Avenue Rd; ⏲most shops 10am-7pm; Ⓢ Bay, Bloor-Yonge)

BMV

BOOKS

21 🔒 MAP P106, B2

The biggest (and most popular) used bookstore in Toronto, with a spectacular selection of titles. Vinyls and DVDs sold, too. It has a smaller second location on Dundas Sq. (✎416-967-5757; www.bmvbooks.com; 471 Bloor St W; ⏲10am-11pm Mon-Wed, to midnight Thu-Sat, noon-9pm Sun; Ⓢ Spadina)

Page & Panel: The TCAF Shop

COMICS

22 🔒 MAP P106, H2

What started as a pop-up for the Toronto Comic Arts Festival (TCAF) has become a permanent comics hub. It's a well-curated store, with excellent picks of Canadian and international graphic novels and designer gifts. (✎416-323-9212; www.torontocomics.com/tcafshop; 789 Yonge St; ⏲10:30am-8:30pm Mon-Fri, to 5pm Sat, noon-5pm Sun; Ⓢ Bloor-Yonge)

West End

For many, the West End is quintessential hipster Toronto, where the city's rich diversity, artfulness, grit and cosmopolitan flair are on full display. You'll find terrific shopping and trendy bars on Queen St W, venerable Italian and Portuguese enclaves along College St, and the rolling expanse of High Park, one of the city's finest urban green spaces.

The Short List

○ **Shopping (p127)** Finding something along Queen St W for everyone on your list, whether it's folk art, cheeky tees or specialty snacks.

○ **Nightlife (p124)** Dancing to live bands and top DJs or sipping cocktails on the Drake Hotel's sweet rooftop patio.

○ **Arts (p124)** Rubbing shoulders with working artists, who enjoy studio, gallery and performance space at the Gladstone.

○ **High Park (p118)** Relaxing in Torontonians' favorite park, where you can cycle beneath the cherry blossoms, go ice skating or take a guided nature walk.

○ **Museum of Contemporary Art Toronto (p122)** Pondering the meaning of contemporary art, installed in a repurposed aluminum factory.

Getting There & Around

Ⓜ The Green line has several stations along Bloor St in the West End.

🚋 Streetcar 501 runs along Queen St W from East Toronto; the 506 runs along College St to High Park.

Neighborhood Map on p120

Maple Leaf Garden, High Park (p118) MANU M NAIR/SHUTTERSTOCK ©

Top Experience

See the spring cherry blossoms in High Park

A favorite among locals, High Park is a verdant, forested expanse with trails, gardens, cherry-tree groves, loads of kid-friendly areas...even outdoor theater productions! The Nature Centre, the hub of organized activities, offers guided walks and interesting events. An engaging and beautiful place, the park showcases another side of the West End.

MAP P120, A1

www.toronto.ca/parks

1873 Bloor St W

dawn-dusk

P

S High Park, 501, 506, 508

Nature Centre

High Park's Nature Centre offers rich programming for children and adults, including workshops and speaker series. A highlight is the guided **family nature walks**, led by experienced naturalists. Walks have various themes – Moth Nights, Oaks in the Urban Savannah, Wild Bees – but all integrate information about the park's ecosystems and flora and fauna. Walks are by donation and usually last two hours. Even if you don't attend a workshop or join a walk, it's worth stopping by the center to get the lay of the land.

Ponds & Creeks

High Park is dotted and lined with ponds and creeks – perfect for exploring and spotting wildlife. The largest, Grenadier Pond, is a great place to see **waterbirds** such as white egrets and trumpeter swans. In winter the pond is used as an ice-skating rink.

Shakespeare in High Park

Shakespeare in High Park (☏ 416-368-3110; www.canadianstage.com; suggested donation adult/child $20/free; ⏲ 8pm Tue-Sun Jul-Sep) is one of Canada's longest-running outdoor theater events, having started in 1982. Guests sit on grassy levels by the amphitheater or – if they pay a little extra and in advance – on a cushion in a premium area near the stage. Bring a blanket and a picnic dinner to enjoy the show like a local.

Don't Miss...

o Shakespeare in High Park

o Guided nature walks

o Cherry blossoms in spring

o Ice skating on Grenadier Pond

o Train rides through the park

★ Top Tips

o If you're visiting in late April or early May, be sure to check out the park's cherry blossoms. The main grove is between Grenadier Café and Grenadier Pond, with more at the Maple Leaf Garden and along West Rd.

o Though tickets to Shakespeare in High Park are by suggested donation, if you pay a set $30 per ticket online you'll score a padded seat near the stage.

o Hillside Gardens is a great place for photos, with small paths, fountains and what seems like an endless display of flowers.

✕ Take a Break

In the heart of the park, **Grenadier Café** makes a welcome pit stop, especially if you stick to basics like burgers and sandwiches; takeout service is offered, too.

For more (and better) options, head to nearby Queen St W and Grand Electric Parkdale (p122), with its hipster vibe and delicious tacos.

E

F

G

H

Barton Ave

Christie St

London St

Northumberland St

Christie Pitts Park

Ⓢ Ossington

Christie

Ⓢ

4 **✕**

17 Bathurst

Ⓢ

Bloor St W

Lennox St

Hepbourne St

Ossington Ave

Bickford Park

Page St

Markham St

1

Kusholme Rd

Dovercourt Rd

Delaware Ave

Concord Ave

Roxton Rd

Shaw St

Crawford St

Harbord St

Jersey Ave

Clinton St

Manning Ave

Euclid Ave

Palmerston Blvd

2

Dewson St

Harbord Park

Ulster St

Dewson St

Montrose Ave

Beatrice St

Grace St

3

20 **✿**

LITTLE ITALY

7

Shannon St

College St

✕

🍽 10

Henderson Ave

Shaw St

Crawford St

Montrose Ave

Beatrice St

Grace St

4

Lakeview Ave

Harrison St

18 **✿**

TRINITY-BELLWOODS

Dundas St W

Bathurst St

Rolyat St **✕** 6

Trinity Bellwoods Park

Gore Valley Ave

Bellwoods Ave

Claremont St

Manning Ave

Euclid Ave

Palmerston Ave

Markham St

5

Foxley St

11 🍽

Argyle St

9 🍴

Trinity Dr

Lobb Ave

Dovercourt Rd

Humbert St

8 **✕** Bruce St

14 🍴

Rebecca St

Robinson St

Logie Pl

Crocker Ave

Manning Ave

Willis St 25

Queen St W

6

22 🔒

WEST QUEEN WEST

23 🔒

19 ✿ **✕** 2

Richmond St W

Mitchell Ave

Massey St

Strachan Ave

Stafford St

Niagara St

Tecumseth St

Sudbury St

Shank St

Stanley Park

King St W

E

F

G

H

Sights

Museum of Contemporary Art Toronto
MUSEUM

1 ◉ MAP P120, B2

Housed in what was once Toronto's tallest building – a factory producing aluminum parts – MOCA exhibits innovative works by Canadian and international artists that address themes of contemporary relevance. Exhibits change four times per year, but all seek to provoke and engage viewers, whether they like what they see or not. (MOCA Toronto; ☏416-530-2500; http://museumofcontemporaryart.ca; 158 Sterling Rd; adult/child $10/free, 10am-2pm last Sun of month free; ⏱10am-5pm Wed-Mon, to 9pm Fri; 🅿🚻; Ⓢ Lansdowne, 🚌306, 506)

Eating

Otto's Bierhalle
GERMAN $

2 ✖ MAP P120, E6

Garage doors, long communal tables, a wide selection of draft beers and ciders, huge platters of brats and schnitzels – it looks like Oktoberfest pretty much year-round here (the only thing missing is the oompah band). A popular spot with an upbeat vibe, this place makes out-of-towners feel like part of the city. Reservations recommended on weekends. (☏416-901-5472; www.ottosbierhalle.com; 1087 Queen St W; mains $10-16; ⏱noon-11pm Mon & Tue, to midnight Wed & Thu, to 2am Sat, to 10pm Sun; 🚌501)

Grand Electric Parkdale
MEXICAN $

3 ✖ MAP P120, C5

Got a craving for tacos? This hip Mexican joint in the West End serves up some of the best in the city, and the wings are pretty darn awesome, too. There's limited seating, so prepare to wait in line for a table; in summer, try to snag one on the gorgeous backyard patio. (☏416-627-3459; http://grandelectrictoronto.com; 1330 Queen St W; tacos $5, mains $12-14; ⏱noon-11pm Sun-Thu, noon-midnight Fri & Sat; 🛜; 🚌501)

NishDish
NATIVE AMERICAN $

4 ✖ MAP P120, G1

Traditional Anishnawbe (Nish) dishes are served at this tiny eatery – more a quick-service counter than a cafe – with two long communal tables. The menu changes weekly, but expect game, beans, and regional fruits and veggies; eg hominy-corn soup, boar omelet, elk chili, wild-rice blueberry pudding and, of course, fry bread. Service is friendly: if in doubt, just ask. (☏416-855-4085; www.nishdish.com; 690 Bloor St W; mains $7-14; ⏱10am-7pm Mon-Fri, 9am-6pm Sat & Sun; 🍴; Ⓢ Christie)

Commoner
GASTROPUB $$

5 ✖ MAP P120, A3

The Commoner is a swanky gastropub in Roncesvalles Village. Lush jewel tones and antique pieces fill the massive yet welcoming space, and the patio is great for sipping craft beer or cocktails on warm summer days. Stop by for dinner during the week or brunch on the weekend. Either way, try the buffalo cauliflower. (📞647-351-2067; www.thecommonerrestaurant.ca; 2067 Dundas St W; mains $13-27; ⏱5-11pm Mon-Thu, to midnight Fri, 11am-midnight Sat, to 11pm Sun; 🚋506)

Pizzeria Libretto   ITALIAN $$

6 🗺 MAP P120, F4

Pizza Libretto crafts what is arguably the best pizza in town. The secret? A wood-fired oven built by a third-generation pizza-oven builder with stones shipped from Italy. Besides certified Neapolitan pizza and other Naples staples, the menu includes a prix-fixe weekday lunch (salad, pizza and gelato for $16) and an all-Italian wine list. Vegan cheese and gluten-free dough available. (📞416-532-8000; http://pizzerialibretto.com; 221 Ossington Ave; mains $15-25; ⏱11:30am-10pm Mon-Wed, to 11pm Thu-Sun; 🍴; 🚋505)

DaiLo   CHINESE $$

7 🗺 MAP P120, H3

Not your typical Chinese restaurant, this chic Asian brasserie is embellished with teal and gold and serves up Little-Italy-does-French-inspired-Chinese dishes. From the fried watermelon to the jackfruit and chili-glazed back ribs, you'll want to try every single thing on the menu. (📞647-341-8882; http://

Best in the West 🍽

If you like to eat, eat well, and eat at the hottest tickets in town, this is where it's at. Choose from a diverse range of restaurants befitting a town where half the population was born outside Canada. Add to that a fresh, hipster spin and – boom! – it's the West End. The top of the heap includes:

- Commoner (p122)
- Otto's Bierhalle (p122)
- Pizzeria Libretto (p123)

dailoto.com; 503 College St; mains $14-48; ⏱5:30-11pm Tue-Sun; 🍴; 🚋506)

Union   FUSION $$

8 🗺 MAP P120, E5

This dandy little kitchen serves a delicious fusion of French- and Italian-inspired dishes that it touts as 'simple done right,' though you could argue that pickled swordfish with snow crab isn't simple. Fortunately, the food, decor and service are masterfully executed, using the freshest ingredients. Steak, chicken, ribs and fish are staples. There's a delightful patio out back. (📞416-850-0093; www.union72.ca; 72 Ossington Ave; mains $15-38; ⏱noon-3pm & 6-10pm Mon-Wed, to 11pm Thu & Fri, 11am-3pm & 6-11pm Sat, 6-10pm Sun; 🚋501)

Bang Bang Ice Cream

ICE CREAM $

9 MAP P120, F5

From burnt toffee to banana pudding, Bang Bang has more than two dozen house-made ice-cream flavours to try. Choose regular scoops, ice-cream sandwiches or bubble waffles with ice cream. Be prepared wait in a long line, especially in summer. (☑647-348-1900; http://bangbangicecream.ca; 93a Ossington Ave; scoops from $4.25; ☉1-10pm Sun-Thu, to 10:30pm Fri & Sat; ☺; ☐505)

Drinking

Bar Raval

BAR

10 ☐ MAP P120, H3

Standing in Bar Raval's magnificent, undulating mahogany interior, inspired by the works of Antoni Gaudí, feels like being surrounded

Local Experiences

Hanging out The 'it' street in the West End is Ossington Ave between Queen St W and Dundas St W – start your night at **Bellwoods Brewery** or the **Ossington**.

Shopping Though there's great shopping on Queen St W, on summer weekends wander north toward Dundas for the terrific **yard sales** that pop up – there are many treasures to be found!

by a set of petrified waves – it's otherworldly. The Basque-inspired *pinxtos* menu is the perfect complement to the surroundings: small sharing plates (squid in ink, smoked lamb belly, foie gras) go well with the list of layered cocktails and fine wines. (☑647-344-8001; www.thisisbarraval.com; 505 College St; ☉11am-2am Mon-Fri, 10am-2am Sat & Sun; ☐306, 506)

Bellwoods Brewery

BREWERY

11 ☐ MAP P120, E5

Fresh, urban-chic Bellwoods pours award-winning beers, from pale ales and double IPAs to stouts and wild ales. With candles lighting up the main room and gallery, the brewery itself is decidedly cool and buzzing with locals. An elevated menu of small plates – cheese boards, chicken-liver mousse, mussels – complements the beers. (www.bellwoodsbrewery.com; 124 Ossington Ave; ☉2pm-midnight Mon-Wed, to 1am Thu & Fri, noon-1am Sat, to midnight Sun; ☐505)

Gladstone Hotel

BAR

12 ☐ MAP P120, D5

This historic **hotel** revels in Toronto's avant-garde arts scene. The Gladstone Ballroom sustains offbeat DJs, poetry slams, jazz, book readings, alt-country and blues, and burlesque, while the Melody Bar hosts karaoke and other musical ventures. The cover varies, but is usually $10 or less. (☑416-531-4635; www.gladstonehotel.com; 1214 Queen St W; ☉5pm-late Tue-Sat; ☐501)

JEFF ROSS/SHUTTERSTOCK ©

Liz Cooper & the Stampede performing at the Drake Hotel

Drake Hotel BAR

13 MAP P120, D6

The Drake is part boutique hotel, part pub, part live-music venue and part nightclub. There's a bunch of different areas to enjoy, including the chic **Sky Yard** rooftop bar and the hipster **Drake Underground** basement. Check the website for the lineup. (☏416-531-5042; www.thedrakehotel.ca; 1150 Queen St W; ⏱11am-2am Mon-Fri, 10am-am Sat-Sun; ☒501)

Ossington BAR

14 MAP P120, F5

With a moody candlelit front bar and a cavernous backroom hosting Friday and Saturday DJ nights, this local fave is a great mix of 20- to 30-somethings who still have a

little life left in them and choose to stray from the mainstream mania. (☏416-850-0161; www.theossington. com; 61 Ossington Ave; cover $5; ⏱6pm-2am; ☒501)

Henderson Brewing Company BREWERY

15 MAP P120, B2

A laid-back warehouse brewery in the Junction Triangle, Henderson has a tasting room with bar, picnic tables and huge fermentation tanks, offering views of staffers at work. Three beers (an amber, a lager and an IPA) are produced year-round; several others seasonally. Check the website for weekly events; there are pop-up eateries on weekends. (☏416-535-1212; https://henderson-brewing.com; 128 Sterling Rd; ⏱11am-10pm; ☒306, 506, ☒Lansdowne)

Après
WINE BAR

16 🚇 MAP P120, D6

Natural wine is what it's all about at minimalist Après. A small, ever-changing menu of shareable dishes pairs perfectly with the low-intervention and ethically farmed *vino* offered. (📞647-292-3317; www.apreswinebar.ca; 1166 Queen St W; ⏱6pm-2am Tue-Thu, to 1am Fri & Sat, to midnight Sun; 🚋501)

Snakes & Lattes
CAFE

17 🚇 MAP P120, H1

For a small cover fee, choose from over a thousand board games, along with local craft beers, milkshakes and shareable bites. Whether you're a Catan player or a Cards Against Humanity fan, there's a game for everyone. Snakes & Lattes has a few storefronts across the city – this Bloor St location is especially popular with University of Toronto students. (📞647-342-9229; www.snakesandlattes.com; 600 Bloor St W; cover $8; ⏱11am-midnight Sun-Thu, to 2am Fri & Sat; 🛜👪; Ⓢ Bathurst)

Entertainment

Dakota Tavern
LIVE MUSIC

18 ⭐ MAP P120, F4

This basement tavern rocks, with wooden-barrel stools and a small stage where you can catch some twang. You'll hear mostly country and blues, plus a bit of rock. Sunday bluegrass brunches (adult/child $7/free; 10am to 2pm) are

Adria Kain performing at Mod Club

a *big* hit – they're tasty, filling and fun, but you'll have to queue to get in. (☎416-850-4579; www.facebook.com/TheDakotaTavern; 249 Ossington Ave; cover $10; ⏰8pm-2am Tue-Sun; 🚋63, 🚋501)

Theatre Centre
ARTS CENTER

19 ✪ MAP P120, E6

Housed in a magnificent landmark building, the Theatre Centre produces and supports experimental works of performance and visual art. Come here to push your boundaries! (☎416-534-9261; http://theatrecentre.org; 1115 Queen St W; 🛜; 🚋501)

Mod Club
CONCERT VENUE

20 ✪ MAP P120, F3

This excellent Little Italy venue showcases alt-rock acts like The Killers and Muse. If you want to flaunt your hip-hop rhymes, look out for 'trap karaoke.' On other nights, DJs play electronic, indie and Brit pop to a packed dance floor. Up-to-the-nanosecond lighting gives way to candlelit chill-out rooms. (☎416-588-4663; www.themodclub.com; 722 College St; ⏰8pm-midnight Mon-Thu, 6pm-3am Fri & Sat; 🚋506)

Shopping

House of Vintage
VINTAGE

21 🔒 MAP P120, C6

Fulfill your one-of-a-kind dreams at this perfectly curated vintage boutique in Parkdale. Known as

one of Toronto's hottest spots for men's and women's unique and designer pieces, this place is bound to have something that fits the bill. (☎416-535-2142; http://houseofvintage-toronto.blogspot.com; 1239 Queen St W; ⏰noon-7pm Mon-Fri, 11am-7pm Sat, noon-6pm Sun; 🚋501)

Craft Ontario Shop
ART

22 🔒 MAP P120, E6

Craft Ontario has been promoting the work of artisans in its gallery boutique for over 40 years. Ceramics, jewelry, glasswork, prints and carvings make up most of the displays, but you could also catch a special exhibition of Pangnirtung weaving or Cape Dorset graphics. Staff are knowledgeable about indigenous art. (☎416-921-1721; www.craftontario.com; 1106 Queen St W; ⏰11am-6pm Mon, 10am-6pm Tue & Wed, to 7pm Thu-Sat, 11am-5pm Sun; 🚋501)

West End Exploring

The West End is a highly walk-able area, and the best way to experience it is to just wander around and explore. Heading roughly east–west you'll pass from neighborhood to neighborhood, each with its own distinctive character and vibe. Lovely High Park marks the area's western edge. When you get tired of walking – it's a big part of town – there's plenty of public transit, especially along the main corridors, such as Queen and College Sts.

Type Books
BOOKS

23 🔒 MAP P120, G6

A lovely independent bookstore with stenciled walls and chandeliers, Type has a little of everything for everyone. The laid-back vibe makes it easy to peruse the volumes (and even take a couple home!), and the colorful children's section is a gem. The whimsical knickknacks make good gifts, too. (☏416-366-8973; www.facebook.com/typebooks; 883 Queen St W; ⏱10am-6pm Mon-Wed, to 7pm Thu-Sat, 11am-6pm Sun; 🚋301, 501)

Public Butter Vintage
VINTAGE

24 🔒 MAP P120, C5

One of Toronto's most popular vintage stores, with everything from clothes to home decor. It's a little overwhelming when you walk in – so much stuff everywhere! – but the odds are you'll find at least one item that you fancy. Plus, the prices are pretty darn good. (☏416-535-4343; http://publicbutter.com; 1290 Queen St W; ⏱11am-7pm Mon-Wed, to 8pm Thu & Fri, 10am-8pm Sat, 11am-6pm Sun; 🚋501)

Châtelet
HOMEWARES

25 🔒 MAP P120, H6

Meaning 'little castle' in French, Châtelet sells shabby-chic home goods with a country feel. You'll see everything from refurbished flea-market finds and vintage knickknacks to whitewashed furniture and whimsical tableware. It's a good place to pick up a decorative gift. (☏416-603-2278; 604 Queen St W; ⏱11am-6pm Mon, noon-6pm Tue-Sat, to 5pm Sun; 🚋501)

Imperative
CONCEPT STORE

26 🔒 MAP P120, C5

'All Vegan Everything' is the motto of this two-level boutique, selling clothes, shoes and accessories made sans animal products or exploitation. Many of the products are created by upscale Canadian brands, meaning you'll find high-quality items with flair. Decent prices, too. (☏416-551-7698; www.facebook.com/VeganImperative; 1332 Queen St W; ⏱noon-7pm Sun-Thu, 11am-7pm Fri & Sat; 🚋501)

Streetcar on Queen St West

Toronto Designers Market

DESIGN

🔒 MAP P120, A6

n the quiet westernmost end f Queen St, more than 30 small lesigners have set up mini studio-storefronts within a cavernous space. It's a mixed bag, but there are plenty of fresh ideas in the pop-ups, which sell jewelry, clothes, and gifts such as beard combs. (☎416-570-8773; www. torontodesignersmarket.com; 1605 Queen St W; ⏰11am-6pm Wed-Sun; 🚋501)

Explore ◈
East Toronto
& Rosedale

East Toronto is best known as a place to enjoy some greenery without leaving the city proper. It used to be a lush wilderness, fed by the Don River flowing through the glacier-carved Don Valley. Over time, the region became farmland, then a factory area and finally residential. Those previous identities – wild, agricultural, industrial – are evident in Evergreen Brick Works and Riverdale Farm. There's also a diverse cultural history in enclaves like Greektown and Little India, a tradition of arts and great food, and even a little hipster edge on Queen St E.

The Short List

○ **Evergreen Brick Works (p132)** Exploring the verdant grounds and community spaces of this reclaimed brick quarry.

○ **Rooftop (p140)** Sipping cocktails and soaking up the spectacular city views at this swanky hotel bar.

○ **Riverdale Farm (p138)** Experiencing life – and chores – on a working farm that doubles as a family-friendly, hands-on museum.

○ **Opera House (p141)** Rocking out to headliner concerts in a historic vaudeville performance space.

Getting There & Around

🚋 Streetcars 501, 502 and 503 connect downtown to Queen St E.

Ⓢ The Green line runs along Danforth Ave, with several stops in East Toronto.

Neighborhood Map on p136

Mars Hotel performing at the Opera House (p141)
SHAWN GOLDBERG/SHUTTERSTOCK ©

Top Experience 📷

Join an eco-workshop at Evergreen Brick Works

An abandoned 1880s brick factory turned community gathering place, Evergreen Brick Works is an environmentally friendly complex that uses its various buildings and spaces to engage the city – there are art installations, live music, a farmers market, a kids' maker space, nature trails, event spaces and more. Come here to experience a slice of Toronto life.

◉ MAP P136, D1

www.evergreen.ca

550 Bayview Ave

free

🕐 9am-5pm Mon-Fri, 8am-5pm Sat, 10am-5pm Sun

🅿 ♿

🚌 28A, Ⓢ Broadview

Gathering Place

Among its many uses, Evergreen Brick Works is a gathering space. In summer there are guided nature walks and eco-focused workshops. Wednesday evenings bring food trucks, live music and art performances. In winter the ice rink opens, street curling is a must, and fire pits are lit for s'mores. On Saturdays a holiday market and cooking demonstrations keep things bustling.

Art Installations

Art is integrated into the public spaces here, most providing a commentary on Toronto's environment. Look for *Native Tenants*, giant native flowers 'growing' near the Children's Garden; *Deep Time*, in the Pavilions, depicting a glacial period 120,000 years ago; and, in Tiffany Commons, *Watershed Consciousness,* Toronto's largest living map, representing the city's ravine and river system.

Children's Garden

An inviting outdoor space, the Children's Garden draws kids in to explore and play. They'll find water features and sand, random loose parts, a garden and greenhouse, even a tipi and quiet zones. Each month there's a theme – waterways, gardening – though most play is self-directed. Staff members are also on hand to provide ideas and help.

Nature Trails

Don Valley Brick Works Park provides 16.5 hectares of outdoor space next to Evergreen Brick Works. Once a clay and shale quarry, it's now a forested park speckled with ponds and creeks, Carolinian trees and a wildflower meadow; trails and boardwalks run through it. For an uninterrupted skyline view of downtown Toronto, head to the top of the east slope.

★ Top Tips

o The Children's Garden is only open to the public on weekends – plan accordingly!

o Rent a bike on-site at Sweet Pete's Bike Shop.

o Learn about the site's fascinating history through an archival photo wall tagged with historical graffiti.

o Parking is in a self-pay lot – and yes, you'll get a ticket if you don't pay.

✗ Take a Break

Refuel at the **Sipping Container**, which serves craft beer and cider as well as organic coffee and fresh juices out of a repurposed – yup – shipping container.

If you want something more substantial, try **Café Belong**, an upscale lunch-and-dinner place featuring locally sourced ingredients.

Walking Tour 🥾

Cabbagetown & City Views

East Toronto used to be all forest and farmland, hugging the banks of the Don River. The area is fully urban today, yet with plenty of parks and green space. Our tour of the area ranges from Evergreen Brick Works, with its paths and eco-activities, to lovely Victorian-era homes and gourmet hors d'oeuvres at the swanky Rooftop bar.

Walk Facts

Start Allan Gardens Conservatory

End Rooster Coffee House

Length 2.8km; three hours

❶ Allan Gardens Conservatory

Begin at **Allan Gardens Conservatory** (p138), located in the oldest park in Toronto. Check out its domed glass ceiling, built in 1910, then continue into its 1500 sq meters of indoor botanical gardens of tropical flowers and rare plants (and warmth in winter).

❷ Cabbagetown

Continue east on **Carlton St**, admiring the change in architecture from modern apartment buildings to Victorian homes as you enter Cabbagetown, named for the cabbages Irish immigrants planted on their front lawns. At **Parliament St** take a left. Walk past little shops, markets and neighborhood restaurants in restored period buildings, and be sure to look up and around: murals are painted here and there on the redbrick walls. If you need a quick break, **Jet Fuel** (p141) is a good place for a coffee, **Salt & Tobacco** (p139) for a gourmet slice.

❸ Victorian Streetscapes

Take a right onto leafy **Winchester St**, admiring the well-preserved Victorian homes Cabbagetown is known for. This is said to be the largest continuous area of preserved Victorian housing in North America, and you'll see beautifully maintained homes in Gothic Revival, Bay & Gable, and Second Empire style sitting side by side, many with heritage plaques describing their histories. Explore **Metcalf St** and **Sackville St** for more Victorian streetscapes.

❹ Riverdale Farm

Meander back to Winchester, heading east until you hit **Riverdale Farm** (p138). A zoo for almost 100 years, it's now a working urban farm. Admission is free, so poke around the stables and fields, learn about pigs at a farmer demo, and maybe even help milk a goat!

❺ City Views

Head east on the farm, down to the foot bridge that crosses the Don River to verdant **Riverdale Park East**, with playing fields, benches and lots of open space. Climb to the top of the park – it's steep – to the charming **Rooster Coffee House** (p139). Turn around: you'll see one of the best skyline views in the city. Buy a brownie, take a load off, and enjoy the view.

A **B** **C** **D**

1

N 0 — 500 m
0 — 0.25 miles

Evergreen
Brick Works ◉

Bayview Ave

ROSEDALE

Glen Rd

South Dr

Park Rd

Mt Pleasant Rd

Sherbourne St N

Elm Ave

Maple Ave

Nanton Ave

2

Dale Ave

Don Valley Pkwy

Castle
Frank Ⓢ

Rosedale Valley Rd

Bloor St Viaduct

Sherbourne Ⓢ

Selby St

Bloor St E

Charles St E

Huntley St

Liuden St

Howard St

Rosedale
Ravine
Park

3 Isabella St

Gloucester St

Earl Pl

St James Ave

Parliament St

Bayview Ave

Wellesley St E

Wellesley St E

Wellesley
Park

Necropolis

Maitland St

Maitland
Pl

Homewood Ave

Sherbourne St

Bleeker St

Prospect St

Amelia St

Salisbury Ave

Metcalfe St

Winchester St

◉1

4

Wood St

CABBAGETOWN

Aberdeen
Ave

✕5

🍴11

Sackville Pl

Sackville St

Carlton St

Riverdale
Farm

Carlton St

Spruce St

Sumach St

Riverdale
Park

Granby St

Church St

Allan
Gardens

2◉

Berkeley St

Gerrard St E

Don River

5

Jarvis St

Mutual St

Allan Gardens
Conservatory

**EAST
TORONTO**

Sackville St

Oak St

Gould St

Dundas St E

Dalhousie St

George St

Pembroke St

Seaton St

Ontario St

Parliament St

Regent St

Sackville St

River St

Bayview Ave

6

Moss
Park

Shuter St

Tracy St

Wascana Ave

Don Valley Pkwy

Queen St E

A **B** Richmond St E **C** **CORKTOWN** King St E **D**

East Toronto & Rosedale

Enlargement

Kintyre Ave

Grant St

Boulton Ave

Degrassi St

Jimmie Simpson Park

Thompson St

9

8

10

13

3

Queen St E

McGee St

12

Broadview Ave

Lewis St

Saulter St

0 ————— 200 m
0 ————— 0.1 miles

Broadway Ave

Cambridge Ave

Playter Blvd

Jackman Ave

Hurndale Ave

Broadview

7

Dearbourne Ave

Fairview Blvd

Wolfrey Ave

Hogarth Ave

Bowden St

Hampton Ave

Garnock Ave

Danforth Ave

Pape

Pape Ave

6

Hazelwood Ave

Harcourt Ave

Cavell Ave

Strathcona Ave

Wroxeter Ave

Frizzell Ave

Dingwall Ave

Carlaw Ave

Donlands

Chatham Ave

Earl Grey Rd

East View Park

Shudell Ave

Blake St

Hunter St

Condor Ave

Boultbee Ave

RIVERDALE

Grandview Ave

Withrow Park

Albemarle Ave

Sparkhall Ave

Ingham Ave

Bain Ave

Riverdale Park East

Withrow Ave

Riverdale Ave

4

Langley Ave

Victor Ave

Simpson Ave

Broadview Ave

Howland Rd

Logan Ave

Jones Ave

Myrtle Ave

Gerrard St E

Munro St

Hamilton St

First Ave

Allen Ave

Boulton Ave

Degrassi St

West Ave

Tiverton Ave

Carlaw Ave

Pape Ave

Austin Ave

Marjory Ave

Galt Ave

Endean Ave

Sproat Ave

Leslie St

5

Dundas St E

Jimmie Simpson Park

Boston Ave

Carroll St

See Enlargement

Thompson St

Colgate Ave

Queen St E

6

For reviews see

	Top Experiences	p132
	Sights	p138
	Eating	p139
	Drinking	p140
	Entertainment	p141
	Shopping	p141

E   F   G   H

Donlands Ave

Sights

Riverdale Farm
MUSEUM

1 ◉ MAP P136, D4

On the site of the Riverdale Zoo, where from 1888 to 1974 prairie wolves howled at night and spooked the Cabbagetown kids, Riverdale Farm is a downtown rural oasis. Now a working farm and museum, it has two barns, a summer wading pool, and pens of feathered and furry friends. Kids follow the farmers around as they do their daily chores, including milking goats and collecting eggs. Visitors can learn about a particular animal during the daily 'Farmer Demo' at 11:30am. From June to October there's also a Tuesday farmers market from 3pm to 7pm. (☎416-392-6794; http://riverdalefarm toronto.ca; 201 Winchester St; free; ⏰9am-5pm; 🅿 🚻; 🚋506)

Allan Gardens Conservatory
GARDENS

2 ◉ MAP P136, A5

Dating from 1858, Allan Gardens is one of Toronto's oldest parks. The highlight is its indoor botanical garden and conservatory, filled with plants from all around the world (and even some turtles in the orchid section). Housed in a stunning, historical cast-iron and glass building, it's a lovely little escape in the city, especially on a cold winter day. (☎416-392-7288; www.toronto.ca/explore-enjoy/parks-gardens-beaches/gardens-and-horticulture/conservatories/allan-gardens-conservatory; 160 Gerrard St E; free; ⏰10am-4:45pm; 🚻; 🚋506)

Local Experiences

Happy hour

The **Rooftop** (p140) is *the* place to enjoy happy hour on the east side. Make reservations – yes, for a bar – or you'll have to wait till after dark.

Farmers market

Instead of heading to St Lawrence Market, east-siders shop for their fresh produce and artisanal cheeses at the **Evergreen Brick Works** (p132) farmers market.

Sledding

Riverdale Park East, in front of **Rooster Coffee House (p139)**, is a popular spot to take a saucer or tube to shoot down its steep hills. Enjoy the view of downtown Toronto, if you can!

Eating

Bonjour Brioche   FRENCH $

3 🍴 MAP P136, H1

The smell of freshly baked croissants will pull you into this little
French bakery-cafe. Inside, a no-
frills dining room bumps up against
glass cases of picture-perfect,
impossible-to-resist baked goods.
Do yourself a solid: order a fresh
salad, then dig into the chocolate
brioche and croissants. Cash only.
(📞416-406-1250; www.bonjourbrioche.
com; 812 Queen St E; baked goods from
$2.50, mains $8-12; ⏰8am-4pm Mon-
Sat; 🚌501, 502, 503)

Rooster Coffee House   CAFE $

4 🍴 MAP P136, E4

Set in a one-time general store,
Rooster is a shabby-chic coffee
shop known for its organic salads,
sandwiches and great coffee.
Street-side tables have the best
city views around. No free seats?
Take your treats and grab a bench
in the park across the road. (📞416-
995-1530; www.roostercoffeehouse.
com; 479 Broadview Ave; snacks $3-11;
⏰7am-8pm; 🚬; 🚌504, 505)

Salt & Tobacco   PIZZA $

5 🍴 MAP P136, C4

A neighborhood pizzeria specializing in Roman-style pies, from the
traditional (pepperoni and cheese)
to the unusual (brussels sprouts
and maple syrup). Gluten-free and
vegan pizzas also on offer. Craft

Summerlicious Toronto 🍽

Be sure to book your tables
in advance for this **culinary
extravaganza** (📞416-392-
2489; www.toronto.ca/summer
licious; ⏰Jul), held at almost
200 restaurants, bars and
cafes across the city. Great-
value prix-fixe menus in three
price categories mean there's
something to suit most tastes
and budgets.

beers on tap and negronis just $5...
what more is there to say? Diners
eat at communal tables in the
small, mid-century Modern space.
(📞647-348-2993; www.saltandto
bacco.com; 521 Parliament St; slices
from $4, pizzas from $12; ⏰11:30am-
9pm Sun-Thu, to 9:30pm Fri & Sat; 🚬)

Athens   GREEK $$

6 🍴 MAP P136, G3

As Greek as Greektown (aka the
Danforth), modern and beachy
Athens serves traditional dishes
made with fresh, local ingredients:
grilled calamari, lamb *kefte* (meat-
balls) and, of course, souvlaki. For
a treat, try the moussaka and save
room for walnut cake. Service is so
friendly it feels like family...diners
are even welcome in the kitchen to
check out what's cooking! (📞416-
465-4441; https://athensdanforth.
ca; 707 Danforth Ave; dishes $8-33;
⏰11am-midnight; Ⓢ Donlands)

Toronto Names Through Time

- Tkaronto
- Muddy York
- Toronto the Good
- Megacity
- The Centre of the Universe
- TO (pronounced 'Tee-Oh' or 'Tee-dot')
- The 416 (also 'the 6')

Allen's
PUB FOOD $$

7 🍴 MAP P136, E2

Featuring one of the city's nicest patio dining areas (in warmer months), Allen's is more than just a pub, although it is a great place for lovers of Irish music and dance. The seasonal menu has hearty, sophisticated Irish fare: cuts of hormone- and additive-free beef, lamb, ale-battered halibut, and curries. (📞416-463-3086; www.allens.to; 143 Danforth Ave; mains $12-24; ⏰11:30am-midnight Mon-Wed, to 1pm Thu & Fri, 10:30am-1am Sat, to midnight Sun; 🚇Broadview, 🚋504, 505)

Ruby Watchco
CANADIAN $$$

8 🍴 MAP P136, G1

Creative farm-to-table comfort food is the game at this homey restaurant, run by two of Toronto's top chefs. (Chef Lynn even stars on the Food Network hit *Pitchin' In*.) A new menu is presented nightly, always four course, always prix fixe. Expect dishes like fried chicken with rosemary honey, and maple barbecue ribs; save room for the artisanal cheeses and decadent desserts. (📞416-465-0100; http://rubywatchco.ca; 730 Queen St E; prix fixe $58; ⏰6-10pm Tue-Sat; 🚋501, 502, 503)

Drinking

Rooftop
ROOFTOP BAR

9 🍸 MAP P136, F1

This rooftop bar with floor-to-ceiling windows and a wraparound patio affords guests a 360-degree view of Toronto and a breathtaking outlook on the city skyline. Shareables and finger foods complement the cocktail and wine lists well. Sunsets are particularly busy. Reservations highly recommended. (📞416-362-8439; www.thebroadviewhotel.ca; Broadview Hotel, 106 Broadview Ave; ⏰5pm-late Mon-Thu, 11:30am-late Fri-Sun; 🚋501, 502, 503)

Comrade
COCKTAIL BAR

10 🍸 MAP P136, G1

Reminiscent of a bygone era, the Comrade is a red-lit bar with a pressed-tin roof, mahogany accents and taxidermied animal heads hung high. The cocktail list is long and sophisticated, and the crowd mostly local. A good place to linger over a strong drink. (📞647-340-1738; www.thecomraderestaurant.com; 1124 Queen St E; ⏰5:30pm-2am Mon-Thu, 5pm-2am Fri & Sat; 🚋501, 502, 503)

FRANCISCO RAMA/EYEEM/GETTY IMAGES ©

Arts Market display

Entertainment

Opera House CONCERT VENUE

12 ⭐ MAP P136, G2

The old Opera House is an early-1900s vaudeville hall. Over the years, rockers like the Black Crowes, Rage Against the Machine, Eminem, Nirvana and Beck have all strutted out beneath the proscenium arch. Today, it's still considered one of the best small venues in town for concerts and DJ dance parties. (📞416-466-0313; www.theoperahousetoronto.com; 735 Queen St E; 🚋501, 502, 503)

Shopping

Arts Market ART

13 🅿 MAP P136, H1

A collective of local artists displays and sells work at this eclectic shop. High quality and unique, there's everything from handcrafted cards and jewelry to pottery and portraits. A few vintage finds, too. (📞416-778-9533; www.artsmarket.ca; 790 Queen St E; ⏰noon-5pm Mon-Thu, to 6pm Wed-Fri, 11am-6pm Sun; 🚋501, 502, 503)

Jet Fuel COFFEE

11 ☕ MAP P136, C4

So arty and grungy, this hangout is for east-end gentrifiers, cyclists and literati who like to jeer at the beautiful people of Yorkville. The best coffee east of Yonge Street. (📞416-968-9982; www.jetfuelcoffee. com; 519 Parliament St; ⏰6am-8pm; 🚋506)

Worth a Trip 🔭
Get drenched on a Niagara Falls boat tour

An unstoppable flow of rushing water surges over the arcing fault in the riverbed with thunderous force. Great plumes of icy mist rise for hundreds of meters as the waters collide, like an ethereal veil concealing the vast rift behind the torrent. Thousands of onlookers delight in the spectacle every day, drawn by the force of the current and the hypnotic mist. This is Niagara Falls.

Table Rock Visitor Centre
📞 877-642-7275
www.niagaraparks.com
6650 Niagara Pkwy
🕐 9am-9pm, to 7pm Sep-May

Horseshoe Falls

The centerpiece of any visit here are the Horseshoe Falls (pictured). Named after their 670m curved shape, they have the highest flow rate of any waterfall in North America; at 65km/h, more than 2574 kiloliters of water per second crashes over the ridge into a roiling **Maid of the Mist Pool**. Powerful and playful, the turquoise waters mesmerize. The prime falls-watching spot is **Table Rock**, poised just meters from the drop – in the summer, arrive early to beat the crowds.

Bridal Veil & American Falls

Rushing waters between Luna and Goat islands create the Bridal Veil waterfall on the US side, just 17m wide. The falls form a perfect, full (and namesake) bridal-like veil that crashes onto mammoth rocks, 55m below. Next to it, the American Falls form an impressive 260m-wide curtain of rushing white water. During the day, rainbows often form in front of it.

The Skylon

The **Skylon Tower** (☏905-356-2651; www.skylon. com; 5200 Robinson St; adult/child $16.25/10.50; ◷9am-10pm Mon-Thu, to 11pm Fri-Sun; P) is a 158m concrete spire with yellow pill-shaped elevators crawling up and down the tower's neck to the top. The interior itself is dated, even a little sad, but the views! Eye-popping and simply picture perfect with the falls to the east and, on clear days, Toronto to the north. The two observation areas – a glass-enclosed indoor deck and a wire-fenced outdoor one – give you 360-degree views of the region. Plus, there's a revolving restaurant and a family-friendly buffet.

Hornblower Niagara Cruises

A classic Niagara Falls experience: **Hornblower boat tours** (www.niagaracruises.com; 5920 Niagara Pkwy; adult/child $26/16, fireworks cruise $40; ◷8:30am-8:30pm May-Sep, to 5:30pm Oct) come

★ Top Tips

○ The second floor of the Table Rock Visitor Centre is a little-known spot for great photos of Horseshoe Falls.

○ The **Niagara IMAX Theatre** offers excellent parking rates – around $10 per day – in front of the Skylon.

○ Niagara-on-the-Lake, one of the best-preserved 19th-century towns in North America, is just 25km from the falls.

✕ Take a Break

An iconic diner, **Flying Saucer** (Lundy's Lane; mains $7-27; ◷6am-1am Sun-Thu, to 2am Fri & Sat; ♿) offers classic eats in a saucer-shaped building.

A local favorite, **Koutouki** (http://koutoukiniagara.com; 5745 Ferry St; mains $22-42; ◷4-10pm Tue-Sun), serves classic Greek cuisine.

★ Getting There

Go Transit (p150) and VIA Rail (p150) offer return services to Niagara Falls from Toronto.

so close to the spectacular Bridal Veil Falls and Horseshoe Falls that you'll be drenched (despite the rain ponchos). Hornblower offers two tours on its 700-person catamarans: a 20-minute daytime 'Voyage to the Falls' and a 40-minute 'Fireworks Cruise' under the fireworks on summer nights with live music and cash bar. Avoid the massive ticket lines and buy a ticket online.

Summer Fireworks

A magnificent fireworks show takes place over the falls during the summer months: huge, sparkling lights and multicolored puffs light up the skies and the roaring falls below. The show starts at 10pm and is held nightly from June to August and on weekends in May, September and October. For a great view, stake out a spot near **Table Rock**, see it from the water on a Hornblower boat tour (p143), or head to the top of the Skylon (p143).

Botanical Gardens & Butterfly Conservatory

Forty hectares filled with thousands of perennials, sculpted shrubs and towering trees make the **Botanical Gardens** (☎ 905-356-8119; www. niagaraparks.com; 2565 Niagara Pkwy; butterfly conservatory adult/child $16/10.25, gardens free; ☉ 10am-4pm Mon-Fri, to 5pm Sat & Sun Sep-Jun, 10am-7pm Sun-Wed, to 8pm Thu-Sat Jul & Aug; P ♿) a visually inspiring stop.

Niagara Falls and Hydroelectric Power

Though nowhere near the tallest waterfalls in the world (that honor goes to 979m Angel Falls in Venezuela), Niagara Falls is one of the world's most voluminous, with over 168,000 cubic meters of water going over its crest lines every minute. At least, that is, from 8am to 10pm during the peak tourist season of April to September.

In fact, the water making it over the falls – Horseshoe, American and Bridal Veil – only accounts for 25 to 50% of their capacity. The rest is diverted into hydroelectric plants on both sides of the border, depending on the time of day and year: Sir Andrew Beck Station Stations #1 and #2 in Ontario and Robert Moses Hydro Electric Plant in New York. Built across from each other, the hydroelectric plants divert water from the Niagara River using a system of gates 2.6km before the falls. The water is run through hydro tunnels on both sides of the border to turbines that generate electricity; the water is eventually returned to the Niagara River, just above Lake Ontario. The entire process is governed under the 1950 Niagara Treaty, an international agreement that assures water levels and a fair division of electricity (Ontario actually gets a little more). Power generated from the Niagara River accounts for 25% of all electricity used in Ontario and New York State – a remarkable figure, especially considering Toronto and New York City are included.

For visitors to Niagara Falls this means that, depending on the time of day and year, the falls may appear more or less voluminous. The highest volume any time of year is from April 1 to October 31, during daylight hours. The rest of the year, or at night, the falls look remarkably smaller but the street lights, somehow, seem to shine a little brighter.

Meander along the leafy paths, passing the parterre garden and the Victorian rose garden with more than 2400 roses. In the center, the domed **Butterfly Conservatory** houses a rainforest-like setting – plants, waterfalls, heat and more than 2,000 delicate butterflies flitting about, often landing on visitors.

Niagara Glen Nature Reserve

About 8km north of the falls is the exceptional **Niagara Glen**

Nature Reserve (☎905-354-6678; www.niagaraparks.com; 3050 Niagara Pkwy; free; ☸Reserve dawn-dusk, Nature Centre 10am-5pm Apr-Nov; P♿), where you can get a sense of what the area was like pre-Europeans. There are 4km of walking trails winding down into a gorge, past huge boulders, cold caves, wildflowers and woods. Park naturalists also offer daily one-hour guided nature walks (11am and 2pm; $7) during the summer season.

Survival Guide

Exterior of the Royal Ontario Museum (p104)
ELIJAH LOVKOFF/ALAMY STOCK PHOTO ©; ARCHITECT: DANIEL LIBESKIND

Before You Go

Book Your Stay

o Toronto has a wide range of accommodations: high-rise hotels in the Financial and Entertainment Districts; boutique hotels in the West End; B&Bs in residential neighborhoods; and hostels that dot the city.

o Summer brings sold-out rooms at premium rates - book ahead!

o A 13% tax is added to room rates; occasionally an additional 4% destination tax is levied.

Useful Websites

Downtown Toronto Association of Bed and Breakfast Guest Houses (www.bnbinfo.com) Select listing of B&Bs.

Lonely Planet (lonelyplanet.com/canada/toronto/hotels) Recommendations and reviews.

Best Budget

Only Backpackers Inn (http://theonlyinn.

Toronto, ON

When to Go

o **Summer (Jun–Aug)** Enjoy gorgeous weather, patio dining and festival season in all its glory.

o **Autumn (Sep–Nov)** Visit for a cornucopia of fall colors and fewer crowds.

o **Winter (Dec–Feb)** Bundle up! Winter brings biting wind and snow but also hockey and outdoor ice skating.

o **Spring (Mar–May)** Celebrate the return of blue skies plus great deals on hotels.

com) Globetrotter fave with a relaxed vibe and loads of spaces for socializing.

Planet Travelers Hostel (www.theplanet traveler.com) Big, central hostel with a great rooftop lounge.

Hostelling International Toronto (www.hostellingtoronto.com) Youthful hostel with theme nights and a basement-level bar.

Best Midrange

Anndore House (https://theanndore house.com) Stylish hotel with city views and a popular street-

side patio.

Downtown Home Inn (www.downtown homeinn.com) Pleasant row house repurposed into a cozy inn in Toronto's main LGBTIQ+ neighborhood.

Annex Hotel (https://theannex.com) Hipster hotel with feel-like-a-local features such as keyless entry and Netflix.

Best Top End

Thompson Toronto (www.thompsonhotels.com/toronto) Chic, design-focused hotel with breathtaking skyline views.

Gladstone Hotel
(www.gladstonehotel.
com) Spectacular
artist-designed rooms
upstairs, and avant-
garde arts and music
scene downstairs.

Drake Hotel (www.
thedrakehotel.ca) Artsy
mid-century Modern
hotel with popular
rooftop and basement-
level bars.

Arriving in Toronto

Toronto Pearson International Airport

**Toronto International
Airport** (YYZ; http://
torontopearson.com; 6301
Silver Dart Dr, Missis-
sauga) Located 27km
northwest of downtown.
There are two terminals:
1 and 3. Check the web-
site to confirm which
one you'll be using to
help with logistics. A
free train connects the
terminals as well as the
Viscount Station, used
by car-rental-agency
shuttles.

**Union Pearson
Express** (UP Express;

www.upexpress.com; one
way adult/child/family of
5 $12.35/free/25.70, one
way on PRESTO card $9.25;
⏱ 5:30am-1am; 🛜)
Direct 25-minute rail to
Union Station, stopping
at Weston and Bloor
stations. Traveling on a
PRESTO card (p151) is
highly recommended:
the $6 rechargeable
card pays for itself
with a return trip to the
airport and is useful for
local transport.

Taxi Travel to down-
town takes anywhere
from 40 to 70 minutes,
depending on traffic.
Fares are $60 to
downtown and $75 to
destinations east of
town.

Billy Bishop Toronto City Airport

**Toronto Islands
airport** (YTZ; Map p34,
A4; 📞 416-203-6942;
https://billybishopairport.
com; 1 Island Airport, Centre Island; 🚌 509) Home
to smaller airlines,
helicopter companies
and private flyers.
Convenient for regional
travel.

**Billy Bishop Airport
Tunnel** (Map p34, A3;
www.billybishopairport.

com; 🚌 509) Looong
moving walkways from
Bathurst St to check-in
counters take just six
minutes.

Free ferry Shuttles
passengers to the
airport terminal in 90
seconds (5:30am to
midnight).

Free shuttle bus Links
Union Station to the
ferry terminal and tun-
nel (5am to midnight
Monday to Friday,
6:30am to 8:40pm
Saturday, and 6:30am
to midnight Sunday).

Union Station

Union Station (📞 416-
869-3000; https://
torontounion.ca; 140 Bay
St; 🚇 Union, 🚌 509, 510)
Toronto's main trans-
portation hub, home to:

VIA Rail (📞 888-842-
7245; www.viarail.ca) Plies
the heavily trafficked
Windsor–Montréal cor-
ridor and beyond.

Amtrak (www.amtrak.
com) Provides long
distance rail service
including to Vancouver
and New York City.

GO Transit (www.
gotransit.com) Offers
commuter rail and
bus service to regional
towns, including Nia-
gara Falls.

Toronto Coach Terminal

Toronto Coach Terminal (Map p80, C6; ☎416-393-4636; 610 Bay St; ⓢDundas) Long-distance bus terminal.

Greyhound Canada (https://greyhound.ca) Runs numerous domestic routes from here.

Megabus (https://ca.megabus.com) Has a smaller, and cheaper, selection of destinations.

Getting Around

Subway

○ The fastest way to get across town, with two main lines: Green (Bloor–Danforth) and Yellow (Yonge–University–Spadina).

○ One-way fare is $3.25/free per adult/child; two-hour transfers included.

○ Service is from 6am (8am Sunday) until 1:30am daily.

Streetcar

○ Extensive service throughout the city, though maddeningly slow during rush hour.

○ Fare is $3.25/free per adult/child; two-hour transfers included.

○ 24 hour; service slows from 1:30am to 5am.

Bus

○ Best for accessing areas outside Toronto's core.

○ Fare is $3.25/free per adult/child; two-hour transfers included.

○ Regular service from 6am (8am Sun) to 1am.

○ Blue Night Network buses provide service on major bus routes from 1:30am to 5am daily (6am Saturday, 9am Sunday).

Boat

○ From April to September **Toronto Islands Ferries** (Map p34, E3; ☎416-392-8193; www.toronto.ca; 9 Queens Quay W; adult/child return $8.19/3.95; ⓢUnion) run to Centre Island (8am to 11:15pm), Hanlan's Point (6:30am to 10pm Monday to Friday, 8am to 10:45pm Saturday and Sunday) and Ward's Island (6:35am to 11:15pm).

○ From October to March, ferries only run to Ward's Island and Hanlan's Point.

○ Book online (www.toronto.ca) to skip the purchase queue.

○ **Tiki Taxi** (☎647-347-8454; www.tikitaxi.ca; 441 Queens Quay W; adult/child $10/5; ⏰9am-9pm Mon-Fri, 8am-9pm Sat & Sun; 🚌310, 509, 510) provides water-taxi service to the Islands. It departs when full.

Bike

○ **Bike Share Toronto** (☎855-898-2378; www.bikesharetoronto.com; 30mins $3.25, 1-/3-day pass $7/15) A city-wide bike-share program that rents bikes in 30-minute increments. Prepare to pay a premium if you fail to dock your bike every 30 minutes!

○ Rentals are around $15/35 per hour/day; bike shops are along the waterfront.

○ City buses have easily loadable bike racks; first come, first served.

○ Bikes are permitted on streetcars and subway trains during off-peak hours only (before 6:30am, between 10am and 3:30pm, and after 7pm weekdays, and all weekend).

Public Transportation Tickets & Passes

◦ Tickets, tokens, day passes and PRESTO cards can all be used on the TTC ($3.25/free per adult/child); they include two-hour transfers.

◦ Tokens are discounted ($3) if you buy at least three.

◦ Day passes cost $13 and are good for unlimited travel until 5:30am the next day. On weekends, one day pass can be used by families or two adults. A great deal!

◦ A PRESTO card, a smart card storing credit, costs $6; convenient if you'll be using the TTC a lot, going to/from Toronto International Airport, or using GO Transit for day trips.

◦ Check the TTC website (www.ttc.ca) for maps and timetables.

Taxi

◦ Easily hailed downtown; also line up outside big hotels.

◦ Metered fares start at $4.25, plus $1.75 per kilometer, depending on traffic.

◦ A tip of 15% to 20% is customary.

Car

◦ Driving downtown is not recommended due to relentless traffic and construction.

◦ Parking is usually $3 to $4 per half-hour in a private lot; reduced-rate parking is often offered before 7am and after 6pm.

◦ Public lots and street parking are $1.50 to $4 per hour, depending on the neighborhood.

Essential Information

Accessible Travel

Download Lonely Planet's free Accessible Travel guides from http://lptravel.to/AccessibleTravel.

TTC buses are all low-floor accessible, and have tools for the vision and hearing impaired. Few streetcars are accessible to the mobility impaired: the 509 and 510 lines are the only routes that accommodate everyone. And only half of the subway stations have elevators.

Lodging is a similarly mixed bag: Modern hotels tend to have elevators, and wider doors and bathrooms, while smaller hotels and B&Bs, many in refurbished Victorians, often do not.

Wheelchair Accessible Taxi Service (https://wheelchairtaxi.online) Provides door-to-door service to the mobility impaired in the Greater Toronto Area.

Access to Travel (www.accesstotravel.gc.ca) Proves information on accessible transportation and travel across Canada.

Society for Accessible Travel & Hospitality (www.sath.org) Tips and blogs for travelers with disabilities.

Business Hours

Opening hours are generally shorter in the shoulder and low seasons.

Banks 8am to 5pm Monday to Friday; some open 9am to noon Saturday

Restaurants breakfast 7am to 11am, lunch 11am to 3pm, dinner 5pm to 10pm; some open for brunch 8am–1pm Saturday and Sunday

Bars noon to midnight Sunday to Wednesday, to 2am Thursday to Saturday

Clubs 9pm to 3am Thursday to Saturday

Shops 10am to 7pm Monday to Thursday, to 9pm Friday to Saturday, noon to 5pm Sunday

Supermarkets 7am to 10pm; some open 24hrs

Discount Cards

Toronto CityPASS (www.citypass.com/toronto; adult/child $73/50) Covers five attractions: CN Tower, Ripley's Aquarium, Royal Ontario Museum, Casa Loma and your choice of Ontario Science Centre or Toronto Zoo. A good deal if you go to at least three.

International Student Identity Card (www.isic.org) Provides students with discounts on travel insurance and admission to museums and other sights. Cards also available for those under 26 but not students, and for full-time teachers.

Electricity

Type A
120V/60Hz

Type B
120V/60Hz

Money

See p22 for further information on currency, ATMs and credit cards.

ATMs

Scotiabank (www.scotiabank.com) provides no-fee ATM withdrawals for members of the Global ATM Alliance. Your own bank, however, might still charge you a fee.

Many convenience-store ATMs charge an additional machine fee, typically $2 to $5.

Credit Cards

Mom-and-pop shops and small markets, mostly in Kensington Market and Chinatown, may be cash only.

Changing Money

To exchange cash, tackle the banks or try **Money Mart** (www.moneymart.ca; 617 Yonge St; ⏲24hr; Ⓢ Wellesley).

Public Holidays

Several public holidays shut down banks, schools, government offices and often many private businesses:

New Year's Day January 1

Family Day Third Monday in February

Good Friday/Easter Monday March or April

Victoria Day Third Monday in May

Canada Day July 1

Civic Day First Monday in August

Labour Day First Monday in September

Thanksgiving Second Monday in October

Remembrance Day November 11

Christmas/Boxing Day December 25/26

Safe Travel

By North American standards, Toronto is a safe city to live in and

to visit, but be aware of the following:

o Yonge St can be sketchy, especially heading north toward Bloor as the strip clubs, sex shops and bars increase in density. Be aware of your surroundings and avoid walking alone at night. Alternatively, walk on University Ave, just west of Yonge.

o At night, Cabbagetown Sth – particularly around Allan Gardens and George St – is iffy. Take a cab or ride share.

Toilets

o Private businesses usually only allow customers to use washrooms and often have a key to enforce this.

o Shopping malls such as the Eaton Centre, and tourist complexes like the Harbourfront Centre, Distillery District and St Lawrence Market, have free public washrooms.

Tourist Information

Ontario Travel Information Centre (Map p48, G4; 416-314-5899; www.ontariotravel.net; Union Station, 65 Front St W; 9am-6pm Mon-Sat, 10am-6pm Sun; S Union) Knowledgeable multilingual staff and overflowing racks of brochures that cover every nook and cranny of Toronto and beyond.

Visas

Visitors to Canada must hold a valid passport with at least six months remaining before its expiration. Visitors from visa-exempt countries (with the exception of the USA) are required to purchase an Electronic Travel Authorization (eTA; $7), before departing their home country. Visitors from non-visa-waiver countries must apply for the appropriate visa prior

---

Dos & Don'ts

Torontonians are a fairly laid-back, friendly crowd and aren't easily offended; however, some rules of etiquette do apply:

Courtesy Please, thank you, and sorry are highly valued words. Use them. Please.

Patriotism Canadians are very proud of their nationality – avoid commenting that they are pretty much just Americans.

Queues While Torontonians usually tut when dismayed, cutting a line can prompt full-on shouts.

Shoes Remove your footwear and place it in the area provided in B&Bs and homes.

Money-saving Tips

o Many festivals are free or pay-what-you-can. Exceptions include film and food festivals.

o Most museums offer free days every month and discounted admission for kids every day.

o Reduced price tickets to the symphony, ballet and opera are often available for anyone under 30.

o Rush tickets to big ticket shows are sold same day and go fast – plan accordingly!

to arriving in Canada. For more info, check the website of **Citizenship & Immigration Canada** (www.cic.gc.ca).

COVID-19

In order to control the spread of COVID-19, all travelers seeking to enter Canada must complete a mandatory health and travel form using the government's ArriveCAN app; it must be submitted no more than 72 hours before arrival. Travelers also can upload proof of COVID-19 vaccination via the app to avoid taking a pre-entry COVID-19 test and submitting to a 14-day quarantine period once in Canada. For up-to-date info and

links to the ArriveCAN app, check out Travel & Tourism Canada (https://travel.gc.ca/travel-covid).

Responsible Travel

Overtourism

o Travel outside the peak summer months (Jun–Aug) to avoid the crowds. Autumn (Sep–Nov) brings crisp days and fall colors; spring (Mar–May) means blue skies and blooms.

o Explore lesser-known neighborhoods (see p17)

Support Local

o Instead of staying in a chain hotel in the Entertainment District, opt for a boutique hotel, B&B or

hostel nearby. Ask about their 'green' credentials before booking.

o Buy local eats at farmers markets. St Lawrence Market (p60) is open year-round, while seasonal markets pop up at Evergreen Brick Works (p132) and in neighborhoods like **Leslieville** (www.leslievillemarket.com) and **Trinity Bellwoods** (http://www.tbfm.ca).

o Support local experts on a guided tour. Try Heritage Toronto (p110) for insight on the city's history or **ROMWalks** (www.rom.on.ca/en/whats-on/romwalks) for a deep dive into Toronto's diverse architecture.

Leave a Light Footprint

o Explore Toronto on foot – you'll see more and better learn how the city works.

o Try biking. City-wide Bike Share Toronto (p150) is convenient for rides under 30 minutes; for more time, rent from a local shop like Wheel Excitement (p38).

o For places further afield, tap into Toronto's extensive public transport system (p150).

Behind the Scenes

Send Us Your Feedback

We love to hear from travelers – your comments help make our books better. We read every word, and we guarantee that your feedback goes straight to the authors. Visit **lonelyplanet.com/contact** to submit your updates and suggestions.

Note: We may edit, reproduce and incorporate your comments in Lonely Planet products such as guidebooks, websites and digital products, so let us know if you don't want your comments reproduced or your name acknowledged. For a copy of our privacy policy visit lonelyplanet.com/legal.

Liza's Thanks

A shout out to the extraordinary LP team: the production crew, my co-authors – I'm so proud to be able to work with you. *Mil gracias* to Mom and Dad for your boundless support, love, and curiosity about places so close to home. Big thanks to Eva and Leo for waiting so patiently for 'Fun... With Mom.' And Gary, my love, there is absolutely no way I could do my job without you. Your support, your understanding, your cheerleading. Thank you, always.

Acknowledgements

Cover photographs: Front: Royal Ontario Museum shown courtesy of Studio Libeskind, mikecphoto/Shutterstock ©; Back: Allan Gardens Conservatory, Inspired by Maps/Shutterstock ©

This Book

This 2nd edition of Lonely Planet's *Pocket Toronto* guidebook was curated, researched and written by Liza Prado. This guidebook was produced by the following:

Commissioning Editor
Angela Tinson

Senior Product Editors
Martine Power, Saralinda Turner

Senior Cartographer
Corey Hutchison

Product Editor
Jenna Myers

Book Designers
Meri Blazevski, Aomi Ito

Assisting Editors Joel Cotterell, Peter Cruttenden, Sarah Bailey, Vicky Smith, Gabrielle Stefanos

Cover Researcher
Gwen Cotter

Thanks to Sonia Kapoor, Kate Mathews, Alison Ridgway

Index

See also separate subindexes for:

🍽 **Eating p158**

🍷 **Drinking p159**

★ **Entertainment p159**

🛍 **Shopping p159**

Index

Our Writer

Liza Prado

Liza Prado has been a travel writer since 2003, when she made a move from corporate lawyering to travel writing (and never looked back). She's written dozens of guidebooks and articles, as well as apps and blogs to destinations throughout the Americas. She takes decent photos, too. Liza is a graduate of Brown University and Stanford Law School. She lives very happily in Denver, Colorado, with her husband and fellow Lonely Planet writer, Gary Chandler, and their two kids.

Published by Lonely Planet Global Limited
CRN 554153
2nd edition – Nov 2022
ISBN 978 1 78868 455 2
© Lonely Planet 2022   Photographs © as indicated 2022
10 9 8 7 6 5 4 3 2
Printed in Malaysia